038083
$15

G000123700

LAUGHING NOW

To Kathy~
from

Fred.

Laugh on!

LAUGHING NOW

edited by

Irene Staunton

Published by
Weaver Press, Box A1922, Avondale, Harare. 2007

© Each individual story, the author.
©This collection: Weaver Press, 2007.

Typeset by Weaver Press
Cover Photographs: Bester Kanyama
Cover Design: Heath Manyepa, Harare.
Printed by: Sable Press, Harare.

The publishers would like to express their gratitude to Hivos for
the support they have given to Weaver Press in the development of
their fiction programme.

All rights reserved. No part of the publication may be repro-
duced, stored in a retrieval system or transmitted in any form by any
means – electronic, mechanical, photocopying, recording, or otherwise – without the express written permission
of the publisher.

ISBN: 978 1 77922 068 4

CONTENTS

AUTHORS' BIOGRAPHIES

DIANA CHARSLEY grew up on a farm in Mashonaland and went to school in Harare, but has lived most of her life in Bulawayo. While she enjoys cooking and walking the dogs, the highlight of her week is practicing with the youth orchestra as a novice clarinettist. Being a late starter, she recently discovered the challenge of writing and though she would like to write more, God, government and grandchildren have other ideas.

JULIUS CHINGONO was born on a commercial farm in 1946, and has worked for most of his life on the mines as a blaster. He has had his poetry published in several anthologies of Shona poetry including *Nhetembo, Mabvumira eNhetembo* and *Gwenyambira* between 1968 and 1980. His only novel, *Chipo Changu*, was published in 1978, an award-winning play, *Ruvimbo*, was published in 1980, and a collection of poetry and short stories, *Not Another Day,* in 2006. His poetry in English has also been published in several South African and Zimbabwean anthologies: *Flags of Love* (*Mireza yerudo*) (1983) and *Flag of Rags* (1996). He has contributed to Poetry International in the Netherlands.

EDWARD CHINHANHU was born in Rusape and grew up in Nyazura. He was educated at Marymount Teachers' College, after which he went to Africa University to read for a Bachelor of Arts degree. He taught in Mutare for sixteen years before resigning in 2004 to further his studies. He completed a Masters degree in Peace and Governance at Africa University in May 2005, and then travelled to The Hague, in the Netherlands for a post-graduate diploma in Governance, Democratization and Public Policy at the ISS. Among his writing achievements are a Commonwealth Award in 2000, an ERA Award (Johannesburg), and a contribution to a compilation of short stories on AIDS published at the University of Cape Town.

SHIMMER CHINODYA was born in Gweru, Zimbabwe, in 1957, the second child in a large, happy family. He studied English Literature and Education at the University of Zimbabwe. After a spell in teaching and with curriculum development, he proceeded to the Iowa Writers'

Workshop (USA) where he earned an MA in Creative Writing.

His first novel, *Dew in the Morning*, was written when he was eighteen and published in 1982. This was followed by *Farai's Girls* (1984), *Child of War* (under the pen name B.Chirasha, 1986), *Harvest of Thorns* (1989), *Can We Talk and other stories* (1998), *Tale of Tamari* (2004), *Chairman of Fools* (2005), and *Strife* (2006). His work appears in numerous anthologies, including *Soho Square* (1992), *Writer's Territory* (1999), *Tenderfoots* (2001), *Writing Still* (2004), and *Writing Now* (2005). He has also written children's books, educational texts, training manuals and radio and film scripts, including the script for the award-winning feature film, *Everyone's Child*. He has won many awards for his work, including the Commonwealth Writers Prize (Africa Region) and a Noma Honourable mention for *Harvest of Thorns*, a Caine Prize shortlist for 'Can we Talk' and the NAMA award for the outstanding book for *Strife*. He has won the Zimbabwe Book Publishers Association Awards on many occasions. He has also received many fellowships abroad and from 1995 to 1997 was Distinguished Visiting Professor in Creative Writing and African Literature at the University of St Lawrence in upstate New York.

ERASMUS CHINYANI was born in Goromonzi, the last born in a family of eleven. He attended St Peter Claver primary and secondary schools. On leaving school, he worked for a printing company and studied in the evening passing both his O- and A- levels in this way. He then took an electric engineering course at the Harare Polytechnic and worked with the Ministry of Construction from 1990-1996. During this time he took a part-time correspondence courses in Freelance Journalism and Short Story Writing. He has had his short stories published in Prize Africa, Horizon and Parade magazines. Currently, he is a self-employed Electrical Contractor and a freelance writer. He lives in Chitungwiza.

JOHN EPPEL was born in South Africa, and grew up in Zimbabwe. He teaches English at Christian Brothers College in Bulawayo. His first novel, *D.G.G. Berry's The Great North Road*, won the M-Net Prize in South Africa. His second novel, *Hatchings*, was short-listed for the M-Net Prize and was chosen for the series in the Times Literary Supplement on the most significant books to have come out of Africa. His book of poems, *Spoils of War*, won the Ingrid Jonker Prize. His other novels, *The Giraffe Man*, *The Curse of the Ripe Tomato* and *The Holy Innocents*, and poetry anthologies, *Sonata for Matebeleland*, *Selected Poems: 1965-1995*, and *Songs My Country Taught Me*, have received critical acclaim. He has also written two books, which combine his two distinct voices, the lyricist and the satirist: *The Caruso of Colleen Bawn*, and *White Man Crawling*. His children's play, *How the Elephant got His Trunk*, is due to be published in the near future.

ALEXANDRA FULLER is the author of the award-winning memoir, *Don't Let's Go To The Dogs Tonight*, which was followed by *Scribbling the Cat*. She was born in England in 1969. In 1972 she moved with her family to a farm in Rhodesia. After that country's civil war, in 1981, the Fullers moved first to Malawi, then to Zambia. Fuller received a BA from Acadia University in Nova Scotia, Canada. In 1994, she moved to Wyoming in the United States, where she still lives with her husband and three children.

PETINA GAPPAH studied law at the Universities of Zimbabwe, Graz in Austria and Cambridge. Her short fiction has been published in literary journals and anthologies in Kenya, Nigeria, South Africa, Switzerland, the United Kingdom, the United States and Zimbabwe. In 2007, she came second in a SADC-wide short story contest judged by J.M. Coetzee. She lives in Geneva, Switzerland, with her son Kush, where she works as a lawyer for the ACWL, an organisation that advises developing countries on international trade law. She is currently completing her first novel and researching for a biography of the Bhundu Boys.

ALBERT GUMBO is a writer and thought-provoking speaker at conferences. He is a passionate advocate of individual and corporate citizenship and is a member of the Hellenic School Council. He lives in Harare.

LAWRENCE HOBA was born in 1983 in Masvingo. He studied Tourism and Hospitality Management at the University of Zimbabwe. He represents a new generation of budding writers who are determined to have their voices heard. Hoba's short stories have appeared in *The Mirror*, *Writing Now* and the magazine of the Budding Writers of Zimbabwe.

BRIAN JONES is a professor of Applied Mathematics at the National University of Science and Technology in Bulawayo and a director of 'AmaBooks publishers.

RORY KILALEA (pen name – *murungu*) was born and educated in Zimbabwe. He has worked in the Middle East and throughout Africa, directing and writing documentaries. His short stories have been nominated twice for the Caine Prize and his poetry and short stories have been published in South Africa, USA, Malaysia, UK and Ireland. In 2005 Rory was one of the award winners for the Africa performance series on the BBC, and his story, 'Zimbabwe Boy', was adapted for the 2005 Africa Festival at the London Eye and then moved to the National Theatre in London. He is also writing radio plays for international radio stations and is currently working on a novel.

DANIEL MANDISHONA was born in Harare in 1959. He was brought up by his maternal grandparents in Mbare (then known as Harari Township). Expelled from Goromonzi Secondary school for what the headmaster called 'habitual truancy', he lived in London from 1977-1992. He first studied Graphic Design and then Architecture at the Bartlett School, University College London. He began writing in 1982 after reading Dambudzo Marechera's *House of Hunger*. His first short story, 'A Wasted Land' was published in *Contemporary African Short Stories* (Heinemann, 1992).]

BRYONY RHEAM was born in Kadoma in 1974 and has lived most of her life in and around Bulawayo. She studied for a BA and MA in English in the UK and then spent a year lecturing in Singapore. She returned to Zimbabwe in 2001. She is currently an English teacher at Girls' College in Bulawayo. She and her boyfriend, John, have a two-year old daughter called Sian.

'There are some things so serious you have to
laugh at them.'

**Niels Bohr (1885-1962) Danish physicist and Nobel
prizewinner**

'Anyone who takes himself too seriously always
runs the risk of looking ridiculous; anyone who
consistently laughs at himself does not.'

**Václav Havel (1936-) Dramatist and first president of
the Czech Republic**

A Grave Matter

Diana Charsley

SYDNEY STRAIGHTENED HIS BACK TO admire his handiwork. He wished he was working on film stars in Hollywood, or at least Cape Town, but coming from a family of engine drivers for the National Railways of Zimbabwe that was unlikely. He had stumbled into this line of work after his father, who was meant to be at soccer, walked into his bedroom one Sunday afternoon and discovered his son dressed in stockings, high heels, make-up, and all. In a roaring rage he informed the whole neighbourhood that no poofter was going to stay under his roof and Sydney was kicked, literally, out of the house, accelerated by the gathered crowd's ribald laughter and useful comments. His mother stood by, wringing her hands. Thus, clasping an armful of bright dresses and silky underwear, with sling-back heels hooked through fingers clutching cosmetics, Sydney left home.

Nursing his bruises and his pride Sydney limped from Barham Green to Belmont where on the deserted street behind Datlabs he found a carton to hold his belongings. From there he trudged toward Main Street and, reaching the Bulawayo Centre, he dallied on the first floor to console himself with a poster advertising the musical, Chicago. There she was: Catherine Zeta-Jones standing, legs astride, revolver in hand, in a clinging, fringed dance dress, dramatically framed by a red neon C. He found himself lip-to-lip with her, gazing at her sensual dark lips and smoky, dangerous eyes. He shivered as he goose-bumped, reflexively imagining himself as Catherine. But his pleasure was abruptly curtailed. A security guard grabbed him by his shirt collar and sent him packing with more insulting epithets.

He wandered aimlessly down the street, thinking about a magazine his mother had when he was about six. In it was a picture of Diana Ross. Mother had gasped when he had grabbed the page and asked her to make a dress for him just like hers. She never told his father about that. Finding himself outside a funeral parlour, he loitered a moment to admire the plush linings of the upmarket caskets. Once more he was startled from his reverie. A spongy man, his face beaded with a coating of oily sweat materialised from behind the coffins. Sydney staggered backwards but the man waved both hands to pacify him and paddled to the door. Then, close beside him, breathing laboriously with garlic-laden breath he smiled greasily, 'Beautiful aren't they?'

'Yes,' Sydney lisped.

'You seem to be a person who appreciates beauty?'

'Erm, yes.' Sydney wished he could sound like such a person. The man stood beside him for a while, staring through the shop window. Then he glanced with interest into Sydney's cardboard box. 'You seem down on your luck?' Sydney did not say anything this time but stared at the pavement. 'I might be able to help you out, you know. There's a room round the back with a bed and a hot-plate you can use if you come and work for me. And I will pay you.' Sydney's delicate disposition was repelled at the thought of working for an undertaker. When he watched movies he avoided the gory ones, preferring Richard Gere romances – how he'd love to be swept off his feet, that is, in the body of Catherine Zeta-Jones.

'Well?' said the man annoyed by the lack of response. Sydney stammered a 'yes'. After all, what choice did he have? His new boss looked pleased and squeezed his shoulder, while letting his hand slide down his back. Sydney squirmed uncomfortably.

The work was surprisingly satisfying. Sydney had a way with grieving families, especially the women who found him safe and comforting, and when it came to preparing a body he enjoyed being alone with a quiet corpse to talk to. For the first time ever he was able to tell another person everything without criticism or judgement. Consequently he treated the deceased with great respect and took trouble getting them ready for their final send-off. With his palette of creams and tints and his eye for detail he restored them to health, so to speak.

His employer had the contract for pauper burials. Even here Sydney treated their bodies with a dignity they were never afforded while alive. He discovered that Tea-tree liquid soap was excellent for masking the sweet, clinging smell that sometimes accompanied them.

His current client (that's what he called them) was the type he liked best: a dowager from a wealthy influential family. In fact, ironically, it was because of the poor that this woman was here. A few months previously, there had been some phone calls over a matter of payment for pauper burials and then a visit from a cabinet minister. After half an hour in the MD's office, the two men emerged, the undertaker looking as if he'd come off second-best while the *chef* looked smug. As Sydney's boss tried to usher him off the premises, the minister took his time looking around and Sydney found him at his elbow as he worked. The great man was impressed. He beamed at the undertaker while he jovially took his upper arm,

'Your wife,' he said giving Sydney a broad wink, 'is very good at his job. Now you'll be able to kill two birds with one stone, won't you?' The MD, smiling and wincing at the same time, took advantage of the physical contact to guide his visitor towards his new 4 x 4.

'If they spent less on luxury cars they might have more to pay me with,' he grumbled, massaging his mangled biceps on his return.

Sydney laughed silently at the memory of his boss's discomfort then turned his attention to the work at hand. No expense had been spared – a white steel casket with gold-plated fittings and a soft pink velvet lining, a designer wardrobe including stockings, black patent high-heels and a haute coiffure wig to disguise the effects of chemotherapy. To this he added his art, plumping the dead woman's withered cheeks with cotton wool and working his cosmetic magic so that when the relatives came for their final farewells they would have an agreeable memory of their loved one. He recalled one family joking that auntie had never looked so serene now that her mouth was shut for the first time in fifty years.

Just as he was calling for the hearse his boss called for him:

'This funeral's top of the range, right?'

'Yes.' Stanley was still monosyllabic with him. It did change to 'No!' with some quick side-stepping when the man tried to come on to him. What made him think that he was homosexual? Didn't he get it that wanting to be a woman was not the same?

'So the casket's spacious with the double lid?'

'Yes.'

'Well bring it to the back, there's something we need to do.' Sydney followed him as he waddled to the next room. Lifting the lid of a ZRP body box, he said, 'See if you can accommodate these.'

'But we can't! Not all three of them!' His boss looked surprised; he had never heard Sydney say so much.

'Just do as you are told,' the undertaker said, abruptly leaving the room.

The service was at Main Street Methodist Church just a few blocks away. Sydney had the casket wheeled to the front of the church and unlatched the upper lid for the purposes of viewing. His client looked as though she was looking out from a stable door enjoying a breath of morning air. Sitting anxiously to one side, Sydney could not bear to look at the family in case he gave anything away. Normally, he enjoyed listening to the mourners admiring his handiwork.

The funeral was long with many eulogies, befitting such an important Amai. The Manyana women in red, white and black rotated between robust singing and wailing at appropriate intervals. At the close of the funeral the family gathered to bid Amai *fambai zvakanaka* and the congregation jostled as they lined up, using the time to catch up with friends. The happy buzz was cut short by a loud bellow that seemed to emanate from the altar.

'We paid a lot of money to have Amai fully laid out! Are you now trying to hide something. Why is this lid sealed? Open it now! Don't you know who I am?'

'He's a cabinet minister,' interjected his wife importantly. Although the *chef* had apparently forgotten their encounter, Sydney was all too aware of who he was up against and had become almost catatonic. It had been just the same when his father yelled at him and called him names. Then, as now, he would freeze rigid as waves of words crashed over him.

'Get your boss here at once and tell him to bring a screwdriver,' the minister bellowed, giving Sydney a push that released him from his spell. He slunk out of the church, the people in the crowded aisles parting like the Red Sea. He wished he could be swallowed up. Once outside he called his boss on the cellphone as he smoked a cigarette, glad to be alone and away from the commotion. The undertaker, realising the urgency of the situation, arrived in no time. Together they hurried up the aisle, the Red Sea parting again.

'Honourable Minister, my condolences,' the undertaker exuded.

'I think there is a lack of transparency here,' the *chef* cut in.

'If my mother was in a glass casket …' She would not cut it as Sleeping Beauty, Sydney thought.

'Honourable minister,' the undertaker squirmed, his ingratiating smile fixed rigidly on his face, 'I assure you that we are professionals and we always maintain the highest of standards.'

'Well then open the casket.'

'Please your Excellency, it is screwed down, the tools are at the parlour. Besides, in the Bible Abraham asked that he should bury Sarah out of sight. This shows that the dead should not be exposed.'

'And people in the Bible also said, none of us will hinder you from burying the dead.' The two eyed each other warily. 'Reverend, find something to open this with.' The pastor, privately annoyed at the upheaval within his church scratched his head,

'There is nothing here Minister, I um…'

'Will this do?' An eager young man burst though the mourners now crowded round the coffin. 'I borrowed this from the repair shop over the road,' he said, sounding pleased. 'I told them who needed it and they handed it over straightaway.'

'Here,' demanded a beefy younger brother of the minister, twisting the crowbar out of the crestfallen young man's hand. Sydney, relieved now he was no longer the centre of attention, hovered at the edge waiting to see how things would play out.

When the one with a neck like a bull prised the casket open the crowd fell back coughing and covering their noses. The sticky smell released from its confinement wanted to embrace them.

'Paugh! What is this?' gagged the honourable minister through his handkerchief. He gingerly peered into the coffin for an explanation. There was something lumpy about Amai's legs under her voluminous skirt. Although he would not dream of lifting his mother's skirt his wife did so without a thought. As she peeled it back she exposed three tiny naked babies nestled against her legs, like piglets latched to a sow. A stifled communal gasp filled the church. The undertaker looked like a glazed ham.

'What the …?' The grieving son turned toward the responsible party as if to hit him. The undertaker did not flinch. With a haughty look and lips set tight he tilted his head back to look down with hooded eyes on the squat cabinet minister.

'Yes, Honourable Minister,' he said sarcastically, 'I was merely carrying out your instruction to bury the poor with the rich; "killing two birds with one stone" was your expression, you might remember. Unfortunately not many people can afford such commodious caskets these days so we have to make the most of every opportunity.' Slamming the coffin shut he strutted off, leaving Sydney to deal with the uproar.

Sydney however had had enough excitement for one day and slipped through the mayhem. Returning to his room he stripped off his morning suit, uncharacteristically leaving it in a heap on the floor. After shaving closely, he applied his make-up deftly before slipping into gossamer underwear with padding in his bra to soften the angles of his body. A clinging fringed dance dress, stockings and strappy high-heels completed the effect. Leaving the vestiges of his past identity, he filled a suitcase with the wardrobe bought with his wages and headed for the railway station. Bulawayo had suddenly grown too small for him.

Minister without Portfolio

Julius Chingono

'STEADY MHOFU STEADY … SLOW DOWN!' It was a harsh command. The Stetson on the woman who sat in the rear fell off her clean-shaven head as the car swayed a little. The contents of her glass spilled onto her lap.

'Oh! My hipster!' The young woman squealed, as she searched in her bag for a tissue.

'Mhofu, what did I tell you … I have a lady here … what's the rush?' The huge man who sat beside the woman slid open the glass partition that separated the passengers from the chauffeur. His white shirt was wet. He steadied his glass to prevent it from spilling again. His voice was tense with barely suppressed anger. The Mercedes Benz slowed down and he hastily gulped the contents of his glass.

'That's better!' The woman defused the tension that was building up in the fat man.

'I'm sorry, *Chef* … I'm sorry.' The driver sounded genuinely sorry. 'It's these potholes.' Mhofu tried to grease away the friction that occasionally occurred between them.

The *chef* watched his chauffeur negotiate the many potholes on the narrow Harare-Masvingo highway and burst out angrily, 'I'm certainly going to make sure that this road is resurfaced without delay … Next month … Mhofu, record that in my memory machine … Don't forget to enter the time and date.' He talked through clenched teeth to impress his female companion and then reclined after closing the small glass window. 'If your trousers are soiled, I will buy you two suits in

7

Masvingo. I like my women to look smart.'

'You mean there are many of us?' she asked, as if she did not mind belonging to a legion of concubines. She belonged to the body of women, hangers-on who were quick to jump into the lap of high-profile politicians and businessmen whenever the opportunity arose. Women who escorted the powerful on their many trips around the country. She picked up her hat and turned to face him. She wore a long white-striped blouse that just reached her knees; maroon pedal-pushers clung to her broad hips and thighs.

'You ... and Maiguru at home. But you ... I love you as much as I love my country. The country I fought for. The country I died for.' He loosened his striped black tie and nodded to his rhetoric.

'This road is just like the one to my home, only better because it's tarred.' She evinced pity for the state of her road just to gauge how the *chef* rated her.

'Where's your home?' he asked casually, refusing to be drawn, but recognising the bait.

'Makoni, Rusape. It's so bumpy that you'd prefer a horse to a bus ride.' She sniffed and sipped while the *chef* mixed himself another drink.

'Which one is this ... not the Nyanga road?'

'The road from Nyabadza to Osborne Dam ...'

'Yes, I know it ... but I wouldn't want to damage my Benz when I'm visiting my in-laws.' He chuckled with self-congratulation. The woman beamed contentedly. She would keep the pressure up, that would give the villagers something to think about. She squeezed his thigh.

'Don't worry .... I promise you that I'll certainly repave the road ... I will do it, that's my job. I was appointed Minister just to do such things.' He slid open the glass partition. 'Mhofu, record, tar the Nyabadza-Osborne Dam road. Do not forget date and time.'

'OK, *Chef*, OK.' Mhofu, who was always addressed by his totem, recorded the instruction without turning his head. The woman thanked the *chef* with a full-lipped kiss on the cheek; and from that day he took it upon himself to spearhead the reconstruction of the road to his girlfriend's home. He determined to adopt the area as his second constituency, finding the prospect of making several trips to the area with his girlfriend in tow quite exciting. Fortunately the local MP was so lazy and ambitious, that he would only relish the minister's visits, implying that they all had something to do with him.

'I will certainly do something about it. That is why I'm Minister. I fought for it and won. But Agnes, how could you ....?'

'Ah! You know my name.' She feigned surprise, a smile playing merry-go-round with her lips. She concluded that if the *chef* took the trouble to remember her name, he definitely had an interest in her. She didn't mind that the relationship would not last. The important thing was monetary gain. She also regarded all her sexual relationships as enviable conquests. She recorded the names of the big guns who she lured into bed in a small notebook. It could come in useful one day.

'Of course I know your name. Can I pour you something more to drink?' The man laughed. 'How can I fail to remember the name of such a beautiful woman?' Agnes preened herself, sipping the little alcohol in her glass like a bee sipping honey. He watched her and was fascinated by her plump, vibrant face which he'd wished to touch since he'd first met her.

'Yes.' She extended her glass to him. They were drinking an expensive imported whisky that the Minister without Portfolio ordered in bulk from Europe. The local liquor made him suffer stomach cramps.

'I knew you when you were abused by that old man ... that Minister of ... you know who.' He laughed triumphantly.

'It wasn't serious', she commented, with scant sense of embarrassment. 'You know it's difficult to say no to people like you ... ministers.'

'I'm glad you are saying the truth ... You are young ... it's these old men who take advantage of you flowers of this country, our great Zimbabwe. You girls who were liberated by the blood of the gallant fighters like us.' Froth bubbled at the sides of his mouth, while he speechified about liberation. He meticulously cleared the foam with his forefinger and thumb. He seemed quite aware of his excesses, and to enjoy his inflated emotions, which frightened those who did not know him well. He performed battle formations and ambushed himself at the rear seat of his Mercedes. 'And that old minister you went out with doesn't even know what the war was like.' He sounded as if Agnes had committed a grievous crime by having a relationship with the old Minister of Human Resources and Labour Policing who did not fight the war of liberation.

'But he used to talk much about the many battles he was involved in during the struggle ... you know that talk ...' The woman knew how to make them jealous. She didn't mind whether what they said was true or not, but she enjoyed egging them on.

'He's a liar!' The minister swallowed the contents of his glass after a loud declaration. 'How can he say that when he cannot assemble a simple AK47 rifle. We want to dismiss all these fake liberators from our government. He was busy collecting degrees when we were dying in the bush.' Agnes could feel the tension of the rivalry but she could not tell whether she was the root of it. She sipped from her glass several times without saying a word, and sighed. He brandished an imaginary rifle from where he sat and fired. It was these military games of his that put his women off.

The Mercedes was speeding again but the tarmac had no potholes. Mhofu juggled the steering wheel as he cruised past the big lorries coming from Beitbridge with their enormous loads, drones and hissing hydraulic brakes. The veld was beginning to look fresh after the first rains of the summer season. Green shoots were sprouting from the charred land and burnt forests, after uncontrolled fires had burnt every living thing. Isolated clusters of mihacha trees sprang into exuberant life here and there on the plains. Munhondo and musasa trees that had survived the bush fires raised their crested heads above the awakening green. In this farming heartland brown soil manifested itself in ploughed furrows over great tracts of land, as the tractors swept across the golden grass. The Minister poured some liquor into his glass.

'Look, see the revolution my girl!' The *chef* unfastened the buttons of his shirt. The speech must have made him extremely hot. He was used to addressing imaginary rallies whenever he happened to find willing ears. 'The fields are red like the blood of our freedom fighters. Soon the seeds will grow and bear crops. The green revolution is in progress. It will bear abundant grain to feed the people. This calls for a toast, my girl. Raise your glass!' Their glasses met, chink, chink.

'To the successful planting season. To the sweat and blood of the sons and daughters of Zimbabwe!' the *chef* pronounced.

'To my new-found love. May the relationship last.' Agnes laughed.

'May it develop into a blissful marriage,' the *chef* rushed on. They drank. The *chef* licked his lips. Agnes kissed him softly. He raised his dark glasses above his forehead like a music rapper and contentedly reclined back in his seat.

'How about some music?'

'Of course, darling.' He slid open the glass partition and ordered,

'Play us that latest Sungura cassette Mhofu.' He closed the glass partition with a snap.

'OK, *Chef*. OK, sir.' Mhofu was a Sungura music fanatic who had in his collection of tapes the latest and the best. The *chef* knew that his driver had a sharp taste for his kind of music, so he sent him out to buy the cassettes. He played the Njerama Boys, a scintillating piece of music that reminded Agnes of her beerhall sprees where juke-boxes played no other music. She clicked her long fingers and nodded to the fast beat as if she wanted to rise and dance. She opened her legs, and jerked her hips sexually towards him. He watched her seductive pelvis revolve, and swallowed. His big palm fell on her thigh and squeezed it. His lips were dry and his eyes fixed on her hips. He again poured the contents of his glass into his mouth.

'Darling Agnes, that is why I fought the war, to win you,' he whispered wide-eyed. 'Where is your handbag?' he asked, but he could see it on her side on the seat. His voice was full of urgency.

'Why?'

'I want to give you something.' He ripped open the zip of the briefcase that lay beside him and withdrew two thick wads of greenbacks. Agnes opened her mouth wide, breathed in noisily and spilled her whisky. The briefcase was tightly packed with stacks of US dollars.

'Sorry dear, I'm spilling my drink.' But she didn't look at the mess. Her eyes remained fixed on the money. She got rid of her whisky in one swig.

'Never mind. Our ancestors in the soil are also partaking of the drops.' He forgot that he was in a moving car. 'Here you are … open your bag.' His big palm shoved the wads into her handbag. 'Do you know where to change the money?' he asked, closing his expensive crocodile leather briefcase with a click.

'Yes, at the bank.' She lied in a graceful voice. She was not the type that would rush to the bank when at the people's market she would get five times more than the official rate. She knelt on the seat, put her arms around his shoulders and kissed him on the lips. 'If you change it at the bank you won't get what it is worth. Where do you live?'

'The Avenues, Sixth Avenue.' She kissed him again.

'I can refer you to some reliable people at the people's market. Be careful … I do not want you to get into trouble. Reduce the volume of the player, Mhofu!'

'I will be careful.' The minister laughed so uproariously that

Mhofu turned to see what had made his master crack. He saw the young woman kiss his boss's forehead as he wantonly stretched towards her. The *chef* caught his stolen glance and shouted. 'You want to kill us? What are you looking at? Mhofu, eyes on the road!' He raised Agnes and pulled her against him effortlessly. Then he slid the glass partition open with so much force that Agnes feared it would fall off its aluminium groove. His big hand was shivering. He gripped Mhofu's nape and banged his head on the steering wheel, seeming not to mind that they might go into the ditch as he did so. 'That will teach you to do your job properly.' He released the unfortunate driver who was struggling to keep the vehicle to the left of the road. The *chef* puffed noisily and shook his oversized head. He closed the glass partition and reclined. Mhofu steadied the car, keeping his eyes glued on the tarmac ahead.

'You frighten me, Mr Kambeu,' Agnes said softly, cupping her empty glass in both palms like a small girl playing with a forbidden ball. Her taut cheeks showed that she'd been genuinely frightened, and in this mood she could hardly address him as darling.

'I'm sorry Agnes … I couldn't control my temper. How can he turn his head to watch us? That's a clear neglect of his duty.' He cleaned the froth from the sides of his mouth. 'You were asking … I am a non-constituency member of parliament appointed by His Excellency because of my war credentials. I am Minister without Portfolio because I can handle any ministry … but why were you asking?' He poured whisky into both their glasses, adding a generous amount of soda water. They were two boozers each showing the other their holding capacities.

'Because you seem to know a lot of things …' She knew how to flatter big-mouthed individuals.

'I can handle any ministry … give me six months and the road to your home will be tarred. Look at the farms … a farmer needs seed, fertiliser and money for labour. I'm fighting for that because the Zimbabwean man is a hard worker who needs help and we are doing just that. Farm after farm is being worked on. Look at those labourers using ox-drawn ploughs … How many spans … eh … ploughs?'

'About six ploughs … no, seven.' They saw people busy on the fields with the onset of the early rains. Some were using hoes. Agnes pointed her long fingers at the workers, mesmerised that men and women could be so absorbed in their work. Women with babies strapped on their backs worked as hard as all the others.

'I enjoy seeing people working on the land as sons and daughters of the soil. I feel my blood flow through my body. I feel rewarded. We only require five years to become the bread-basket of the whole region. I like farming. Do you know how many farms I have? Five! And I'm in the process of acquiring others. I can get you one … your size.' He chuckled triumphantly. Agnes raised her shoulders to indicate that she was not interested in farming. 'You don't do the dirty work … you get a farm manager.'

'I don't want to live in the woods.'

'Look at those lazy bastards.' They were travelling past a farm compound of about twenty houses. 'Look at the women plaiting each other's … hair! Can you expect anything from such people? The fields are still forests covered with grass and bushes. Are they not ashamed?' Women sat on the verandahs of small brick houses facing the road; dilapidated farm dwellings that clearly needed thorough refurbishment.

A group of boys stood around their friend who was digging with a hoe. It was evident that they were digging for something they regarded as important.

'Aren't they supposed to be at school?'

'They are … some of these land-owners do not care about the welfare of their workers. There must be a school at every farm.' The *chef* clicked his tongue angrily.

'They are digging for mice … hunting mice.' Agnes laughed, her small face at the mouth of her glass, to the disappointment of the *chef* who looked out of the window fantasising and grunting.

A few miles further on, at the next farm settlement, men and women were dancing and drinking beer. They even raised their beer mugs and shouted 'Cheers' to passing motorists. The convergence of people was quite large considering the number of matchbox-size houses along the neglected fence that ran parallel to their route. Away from the compound another group of men squatted in a ring, playing cards. They pointed at each other and shouted angrily. There were more bad losers than winners. They passed another compound that looked deserted and the land lay fallow.

'This is prime land with the best soil … the white man did not want to leave … We had to invade the farm with truckloads of youths and remove him forcefully. Now our people are wasting it like this. Some people do not realise that many cadres died for the country … for the land.' The minister consoled himself with a few more swigs, gulping in his haste to continue with his discourse. Agnes looked away. She did not want to encourage him by pretending to be attentive. She did not enjoy political speeches. She found relationships with politicians profitable but tedious because they forgot that she was a girlfriend and not a women's league chairwoman. She wanted to listen to music and not tirades about land. This was one thing she found wearisome about her profession. She wanted to entertain her boyfriends but some of her clientele was too egoistic to let her perform her duties. She found politicians bombastic. Most of them thought that she was naïve. She let them believe so by not talking much and pretending to listen.

'I think we have to repossess this farm and give it to someone willing to use it profitably. We cannot allow such disrespect for policy to ruin our national agenda. The revolution we are going through is the green revolution.' His thick finger slid open the partition. 'Mhofu, book this farm for repossession ... we are in the Beatrice area ... is it not so?'

'Yes, sir.' Mhofu recorded the instruction. He was excited that he also boomed instructions into the recorder, a thing normally done by the *chef* who was on that particular day not interested. Mhofu temporarily forgot about his boss's fit of temper and his still sore neck.

'Nothing – nothing really.' She was not listening. Her mind was in her handbag. Agnes was anxious to know what the bundles were worth, but it was not the right time to drift because the *chef* was talking. She brought herself back to reality; she *had* to listen to please the minister. Payment for listening was in foreign currency. She sat tilting her head towards him, her half-filled glass cupped in her hands and tried to be attentive, though all the whisky was making her sleepy.

'In such circumstances we are excused to think otherwise ... I mean we suspect sabotage ... sabotaging the revolution. How can a son of the soil leave the land to lie fallow. How can ... I think Mhofu knows.' He slid open the partition window again. Mhofu turned to listen, slowing down the Mercedes Benz.

'Do you know the owner of this farm?' The pattern of idleness repeated itself at the farm compound. The drunkenness manifested itself at all compounds. People really enjoying their alcohol and prostitutes seemed to have found themselves appropriate working places to sell their wares. Life seemed a long celebration. Women danced and wriggled their hips, sexually taunting the motorists. The men whistled, raised their mugs and beckoned them to join in the partying. And all these scenes of gambling and drinking men provoked the *chef's* ego: he was, after all, a revolutionary who always repeated that 'he died for the country'. Mhofu did not answer immediately. 'Mhofu, don't you know?'

'I know. Are you also forgetting?' Mhofu fixed his eyes on the road ahead.

'I do not remember … whose farm it is?'

'It is e – e – e – don't you remember?' Mhofu smiled to himself and turned back when he had straightened his face. He bit his lower lip and shouted at the top of his voice. 'It is yours, *chef*.' He turned and gave his full attention to the road ahead.

'What are you saying?' Mhofu was not sure whether the *chef* heard him or not. But he was not up to something sinister.

'It is your farm, sir.' Mhofu sounded genuine, but a vengeful urge was rising inside him. 'It is yours.'

'My farm how? I have five remember. He began to tick them off on his fingers.'

'You remember we came here and drove away the white owner who lived on the hill across a small stream one and a half kilometres from this road … We have passed the turn-off. We were with some youths and a woman comrade you drank with at the Mvuma Hotel.' Mhofu was eager to make him remember. Suddenly, he saw an opportunity to shame the man who forever bullied him. His protection lay with Agnes. He has a witness. He knew that the farm was not the only one that supposedly now belonged to the *chef*, which lay fallow.

'You mean … oh … it is for that woman, damn woman's league secretary.' The *chef's* voice was so hollow, it seemed loud in his ears. 'It can … not be … my farm … *That woman* …' He did not finish his statement. He instead finished his half glass at one gulp and poured some more which he drank without dilution. 'Play me some music, Mhofu.' He slammed the window partition shut.

The Chances and Challenges of Chiadzwa

Edward Chinhanhu

WITH ROADBLOCKS MOUNTED ON ALL MAIN ROADS out of and into the Chiadzwa area of Marange District in Manicaland Province, there was little chance of anyone smuggling out the recently discovered diamonds without detection. Large numbers of soldiers, plain clothes and uniformed policemen and women were deployed throughout the district. Fifteen police officers had already lost their jobs for being discovered in 'deals'. Even the selection of the officers manning the roadblocks was now carefully done, to ensure that only those with a proven record, principles, and loyalty to the government were posted on roadblock duty, for which they received special incentives and privileges. They were thus very zealous and carried out their duties with boring thoroughness, making sure that no diamond illegally left Chiadzwa. They also kept an eagle eye on each other, for trust was in short supply.

The Marange District itself, in which the village of Chiadzwa is located, is one of the driest in the country. Very few crops do well, and even the so-called drought-resistant ones such as *rapoko* and *mhunga* barely survive. When they do, birds, locusts, mice, baboons and other wild creatures wreak havoc on them, leaving very little to harvest. Only the oldest men and women of the district, those in their eighties and nineties, could reminisce with nostalgic smiles about one or two 'real' harvests, and they were many, many years ago. Later generations knew nothing but strife, struggle and starvation. The few who could afford radios *and* batteries to power them heard government ministers talking year after year, of bumper harvests, and the promise that nobody would die of hunger in Zimbabwe. This made most wonder whether such eminent persons lived in the country or not; indeed, from time to time, they might attend the burial of a hunger victim, but statistically, such corpses were classified as having died of AIDS.

During the endless rallies and meetings at election time, promise upon promise was made, about how the people's government would introduce irrigation schemes, and how convoys of trucks would roll into the district, filled to the top with food to give the people, for free. To begin with, the *povo* had fallen for this gimmick, but soon realising they'd been taken for a ride, had voted for the opposition. This led to violent reprisal, so they had stopped voting altogether. Surprisingly, however, the ruling party candidates continued to win, with a 'heavier' and 'heavier' majority each time.

Nonetheless such majorities did not affect the people's daily lives in any way. Silently, life continued; the lucky ones watched their kinsmen being born, grow and die, just like the crops they buried in the dry sand.

Then, suddenly, just like the proverbial bolt from the blue, the heavens smiled upon them. From nowhere, like manna from heaven, diamonds were discovered in an area of the district called Chiadzwa. Diamonds! Just like that!

With the first successful, clandestine sale, the news spread fast, and in no time the whole village awoke from its slumber. Like a disturbed nest of ants, the district was abuzz with life. Men and women, young and old, strong and weak, able and disabled, all joined in the frenzied search for the precious mineral. Schoolteachers and their pupils abandoned classes and fled to the mountains, where, shoulder to shoulder, they jostled for space. Nurses and other government workers filled in sick-leave forms and traded the tools of their trade for picks, hoes and shovels. There was animation everywhere. To start with, everyone searched for the clear type of diamond, which quickly assumed the name of 'glass'. It fetched a lot of money, particularly from buyers in Mutare and Harare. The market soon grew to include South Africa and Mozambique, and this brought a further growth in the price.

People from other places arrived, and within a few weeks of the discovery, the district was awash with strangers. It was rumoured that even the so-called political heavyweights, from members of parliament to government ministers, were involved. This, however, did not seem to matter much, because still more diamonds were discovered. They seemed to materialise from everywhere. Even a slight scratch of the ground would reveal a 'glass'. Another variety of diamond was also discovered, but it was of inferior quality. The villagers called it the 'ngoda', though commercially it was known as the 'industrial' variety diamond.

Then the meetings started. At first, the government said it wanted to bring order to the mining process. They talked about environmental degradation, soil erosion, and so on, ponderous words which confounded the villagers. A few days later, a series of other closed meetings took place, and soon after, the police and army moved in. The whole area was declared government property, and only the Ministry of Mines had the authority and right to carry out mining operations. There was heavy resistance, but more and more armed policemen and soldiers were brought in. They set up roadblocks on all roads into the district, and carried out patrols on horseback. Vicious dogs accompanied them. Many people were beaten to a pulp, others were shot, and their diamonds seized, the luckier ones were thrown into jail for five years. It was rumoured, however, that two or three ministers still continued to mine unabated.

Brought to their knees once again, the villagers were left wondering. They had had a taste of the sweet things that money could buy. Some had destroyed their pole and *dagga* huts, to build new ones, which they roofed with asbestos sheets. Others had furnished such houses, they had bought solar panels for electricity, radios, television sets and other luxuries. Some had acquired goats (the only 'useful' drought-resistant animal in the district), which their children rounded into pens on brand-new bicycles – in other words, dreams made manifest. The more adventurous had started businesses, while others had translocated to the city of Mutare, where they had bought brick homesteads. The school and local clinic had been renovated, and some teachers, nurses and other formally employed people moved around in smart new cars. Music blared non-stop from the shopping centre, and plans were underway to build a recreation centre for all villagers. There was even talk of harnessing water from the nearby Odzi River, for irrigation purposes. When the people mentioned all these plans to the political authorities, they were told that their government would do everything for them, but not now ...

Disillusioned but patient, the villagers waited. Slowly, the hunger of old began to creep in again. Their brains began to work. They knew that once they managed to escape the soldiers and police on patrol, and eventually the roadblocks, they were on the home run. It was never difficult to find buyers. Moreover, the stones had multiplied several times in price. Whereas a gramme of *ngoda* had previously been between thirty and forty thousand dollars, now it fetched between three and four hundred thousand – even more. A gramme of glass could fetch you between three and four million. The higher the risk, or the scarcer the commodity, the higher the price.

Lured by these high prices, the villagers began to smuggle the diamonds out. At first they hid them in shoes, socks, and underwear, sewed them into the hems of their clothing, poked them into their hair, or their wigs, then in loaves of bread, under motor vehicles, in the mouth, and anywhere else they thought might be safe. A lucky few escaped, but others got caught and barely lived to advise their neighbours against trying. The police and soldiers became more brutal with each arrest.

It was against this background that some elders of the village met one night to discuss what to do. Only four or five of the oldest families in the village were represented. Several other younger men in their forties and fifties were there as well. They had been carefully selected for their bravery, and more particularly for their outspokenness at rallies and meetings. The Headman of the village was not invited, for political reasons. This meant that the meeting was held in the strictest confidence, and every man present had to swear his allegiance to the bald-headed man with a long white beard, sitting on a wooden stool at the far end of the hut. Every villager knew him only as Magwegwe. He was old, poor and obscure, but slow and deliberate in his actions. He also never talked much, but was in the habit of shaking his head every time he heard something he thought puzzling or downright stupid. On the rare occasions when he grew excited, he talked about his heyday, a period when he had lived and worked in Magwegwe, a suburb of Bulawayo, and of the son he had fathered there. He had never married, and as far as every villager was concerned, he was simply a fixture, a solitary figure who lived quietly alone on the outskirts of the village.

After counting the heads in the hut, the old man gave a short speech which took almost everyone by complete surprise; taking full advantage of their perplexity, he continued: 'So everything is in your hands, to be brave and save your fellowmen, or be cowardly and watch them die one by one as before.' He paused, then in an almost inaudible, but still clear, voice, he continued: 'As for me, I have nothing to lose. I do not have any longer to live. I've had my good times and my bad and I can't complain. A lot of my contemporaries died without witnessing these diamonds, and I consider myself privileged to have at least seen them. It is God-given wealth. God has heard our cries over the years, and gave these stones to us. But now look …' He swept his arm left and right, his eyes piercing into those of his audience. They all hung their heads and looked away under his challenging gaze.

They continued the discussion deep into the night, arguing in hushed voices, until the crow of the first cock, then they dispersed, one by one, each to his home.

A week passed, and another, and then the meeting was convened again.

'Let us hear what you have brought back,' Magwegwe said challengingly.

There was another brief silence, then one man cleared his throat, and spoke. 'Sekuru, the people you sent me to see are all in perfect agreement with the plan. They can't wait to implement it. They are eager to know the date of its execution.'

'All right, Matumbu. What about you, Dzobo?'

'Same as mine, Sekuru. They can't wait. In fact, it was all very easy. I didn't even have to convince them. It appeared they'd been waiting for just such an idea.'

Eight other men were asked the same question, and they each echoed the same approving sentiments.

'All right then,' said the *sekuru*, for once looking happy. 'It seems the stage has been set. Now, tell me when?'

Almost at the same time, all the men said, 'As soon as possible!' This pleased the old man, and his creased face deepened into a half smile, before continuing with faked incredulity, 'As soon as possible? But we don't have anything, yet. Nothing!'

'That can be arranged, Sekuru,' said a middle-aged villager. 'It's not difficult to send someone to town to buy everything that we need.'

'Indeed!' several others agreed at once.

'OK then,' the old man said again. 'Who shall we send to town?'

A sixty-year-old volunteered. 'I can go, provided one youngish man and an elderly woman accompany me. We also need a vehicle, preferably a truck.'

'Muza said we could include him in the plan,' added another.

Muza was a businessman at the shopping centre, and he owned a *bakkie*. But then somebody thought it was not safe to use a local truck, and so it was suggested that one be hired from Mutare. Muza's truck would be used later. Two million dollars was set aside for hiring it. There was further discussion of the finer details, and then the meeting ended.

Three days later the village woke up to the announcement of the death of Magwegwe. The news was received with indifference by most people, many of whom went about their business as usual. Others, out of courtesy, paid a brief visit to his hut, but left most of the work to the menfolk of the village, for he was a bachelor. For the same reason the Headman also did not attend, but sent a representative. Burial had to be delayed by a day, because news had arrived that the old man indeed had a son, who had indicated that he had to be present at his father's burial. People were surprised when they saw him, and wasted no time in gossiping about today's children who ignore their aged parents. The young man looked quite well-fed and successful. He further surprised some mourners when he said that though he still lived and worked in Bulawayo, he had built a new home near the border with Mozambique, and wished to take his father there for burial. This was debated for a while, and it was finally agreed that there was nothing wrong with his request. The police were informed, and clearance was given. At around ten o'clock that same morning, an open truck arrived from Mutare carrying a coffin. Ten or eleven men put the old man inside, and soon, the truck was on its way out, with the men at the back singing a soft, mournful dirge.

At the roadblock, the police and soldiers stopped the truck.

'Get out, everybody!' said a young sergeant.

The men all jumped out of the truck, their faces long and sombre. They were ordered to stand in a line, one behind the other. Thirty soldiers came upon them, and began to carry out a thorough search. They were groped from top to bottom. The two women with them were also searched by each of eight women constables who wore gloves, and groped their private parts. Meanwhile, more policemen and soldiers were combing the whole truck, searching in, over and under it.

After what seemed an eternity, the sergeant ordered that they drive off. Silently and unhurriedly, the men and women jumped on and the truck went through the booms, and out onto the tarmac. About five kilometers on, it changed course and took a dirt road into a small forest, in which it travelled another three or four hundred metres before stopping. Everybody jumped out, and two men unscrewed the coffin, then flipped open the lid.

The old man remained still, his arms smartly crossed on his chest. His sudden wink was accompanied by a twist of the mouth, and sent everybody into stitches of laughter. He rose up, and diamonds fell from all over him – from inside his smart funeral jacket, the new shirt, and the cloths in which they had wrapped him. When he got out of the coffin, more diamonds covered the base of the coffin, mostly the 'glass' kind, but with some *ngodas* as well. There were subdued but excited handshakes and clapping from those around him. Everyone patted him with awe and congratulation that his plan had worked. He did not say anything, but continued to smile, shaking hands with the young man, and everyone else. The former, who was actually a diamond-buyer, went to a rock nearby and pulled out a tightly packed rucksack, similar to the ones in which school children carry books. He said, 'Here is exactly the amount we agreed upon. Your friends here counted it with me – US$500,000 plus Z$44,000,000.' Some doubting Thomases thought they could count it, but midway through they abandoned the exercise. There were just too many notes. Everything settled, the young man took his loot from the coffin, stowed it into bags and pockets, and took the old man with him. It had been arranged that he return to Bulawayo, where a home had been bought for him, and servants arranged. The villagers took their money, to be shared equally among themselves later, before each thought of where to spend the next few nights. But first, they had to bury the empty coffin, which they did with a pomp and glee rarely seen at a 'funeral'.

Last Laugh

Shimmer Chinodya

At the gate she nearly collided with a cat strapped up in a white bandolier. Two scrawny dogs were alternately courting and kissing with their cordless snouts, or sniffing in the half-light for condoms among food scraps, waste paper and garbage. Trying to make love at the foot of a hill of demolished brick and mortar, they were eager to beat the curfew of daybreak, after which children and grown men would surely – spitting with half-savage glee – kick them to separate them from their lustful union, or curse them away with stones.

As if the human race never made love! Or, better put, as if the human race never engaged in sex. She imagined the National Sports Stadium packed with people all rising and shouting 'Gooooal!' Where did they all come from? All those thousands of people, those zillions of humanoids swarming the streets of the world, if not from the same seedy, sticky, smelly depths of the human anatomy? How much sniffing, moaning, grunting and coming had gone into their individual making? How much gasping and clasping?

Funny, she thought, how in these cramped, sleep-suffused rooms couples were nakedly, heatedly, disentangling from each other with nothing and no one to whip or kick them apart but the stark fact of their disparate lives; groping and fumbling in dazed hordes to face the new day. Outside bathroom doors, voices in the frantic queues were urging, 'Hurry up in there, Auntie! This is not a maternity ward. Are you giving birth to quads or skinning a pig or what?'

But now, with her husband having half deserted her for Botswana (to look for a job, so he said) and her two children packed off to her mother in her village, (cheaper schools, simpler meals, no transport fares and more room to play in – plus God's fresh country air, of course) all she'd done over the last three years was work and work every day to fend for her family and her ageing mother.

Half-buried in the rubble, a sign read: PRAIVET PECKING, KEEP OFF THE LONE PRIZ, though there was hardly a blade of grass in sight. Down the street, in a chicken-run as yet un-touched by the demolition crews, a lone rooster crowed, belatedly, 'Kukurigo-rigo'. From behind a hedge, a tramp yelled, 'Rigo, rigo your mother's! We're up already, idiot.' Spotting her, the man hastily buttoned up his trousers, straightened his cap, stood to attention and said, 'Sorry, Mai George. I didn't hear you coming. Eh, eh, excuse the language. Please do proceed.'

At the Home Industries Centre, or what remained of it, among gaping walls, smashed windows, mangled door-frames and torn roofs, a few surviving signs brazenly announced:

> MAI IVY, ENTER-NATIONAL 'MAZONDO' WITH FULL (MUTI) FOR TYRED BACKS
> FRESH EGGS LAID HERE WHILE YOU WATCH.
> KWALFIED HARE-DRESSER, FRY YOUR HEAD QUICK!
> CAR-PANT-RY – ODROBS, SOLFAS, CHAIRS RAPED HERE
> GOBLINS BOUGHT AND SOLD INSIDE – ALL SYZES AND AIGES

Under the eggs' sign an enterprising customer had scribbled, 'Have you tried to sing to the hens?' Under the goblins' advertisement another had added, 'Do you also sell Maenza lightning from Mutare?'

There was already a sizeable queue at the bus-stop. A *kombi* bursting with human cargo squelched to a halt to pick up a few frenzied passengers then idled, swaying like the back of an elephant. An elderly couple scrambled in. Mai George squeezed in past the red-eyed, wild-haired *hwindi*. The bald man sitting next to her said, to no one in particular, 'Gehena is better, don't you think – there you don't have to spend any money on firewood.' Another man two seats ahead cut in, 'Yes, but there'll be a lot of gnashing of teeth.'

A toothless old woman blabbered, 'Thath doesnth conthern me.'

'Not so fast, *gogo*,' chirped the bald man. 'Everyone without teeth

24

will be provided with a brand new set. And there won't be any Razaro to bring a drop of water.'

'No sacrilege meant,' coughed yet another, 'but I think hell is where all the real people will congregate.'

The *hwindi* clutched at the sheaf of notes between his lips, like a cat grabbing a flaccid mouse, his body rocking with the jerking bus. The fare had gone up again – a daily event. The young man swung into action, 'Heaven or hell, pay up, parents. The fare is like a snake – it has no reverse gear,' as he stuffed the notes into a paper bag.

In the *kombi* the speakers were turned up to maximum volume. Hosiah Chipanga's blaring voice was counselling his fans in Shona:

BEER IS OK – IT DOESN'T INTOXICATE TEE-TOTALLERS
THE PUB IS OK – IT NEVER VISITS YOUR HOME
KANA JERE RAKANAKA HARIMBOKUSINGI …

As if in competition, another kombi passed by, in the opposite direction, with Xtra Large chanting:

(I LOVE YOU, I LOVE YOU. COME STAY WITH ME AT OUR HOUSE)
MY FATHER HAS A MACHINE WHICH BENDS BANANAS
AND *VANE KAMWE KAMUSHINA KANOITA* ADD *VANA VEMAZAI MUMAKANDA ACHO*
(I LOVE YOU SO MUCH) I COULD CHEW THE TAR OFF THE ASPHALT ROADS
AND MAKE THE D.D.F. COMPLAIN

***

At the supermarket her favourite butcher winked at her and said, 'Meat has gone up again, Mai George. Before they year is out, we'll be stewing each other. *Zvatsuro nagudo. Sekuru huyai tibikane. Sekuru ndatsva ndatsva.* Human goulash, a la carte. Or, as my grandfather used to say, back in the days of loincloths, "We will dine on *dhaka nejecha*."'

She ordered cow and pig trotters, offal, ration beef, fish, *madora* and a medium-sized bag of mealie-meal. At the till, the operator, who was one of her faithful lunchtime customers, said, 'Mai George, have you heard about the farmer who bought wheelchairs for his pigs?'

'Why?' she inquired dryly.

'Because his wife loves pigs' trotters.

'Oh.' Mai George had heard all the jokes before. People loved to laugh and hold the world at bay.

'And did you hear about the evil – sorry – civil servant who tried to organise a demonstration against the Governor of the Reserve Bank?'

'Why?'

'He was so broke he wanted the governor to reinstate the three zeros on the new currency.'

'Really?'

Did you …? Did you …? Did you? Mai George smiled obligingly, loaded her purchases into an old sugar bag and lugged them to her open air 'kitchen' under a *muunga* tree at the back of the industrial sites. She retrieved her kitchenware from a friendly garage and got her pinewood fires going. For hours she was boiling, stewing, frying, stirring and ladling.

Her customers were a pretty mixed lot, most of them from the surrounding industrial zones – motor mechanics, glaziers, garage attendants, electricians, cobblers, plumbers (did the latter ever thoroughly wash their hands, she wondered; was it possible to scrape out the grit from underneath their fingernails, to rinse the dirt out of their lives?) There was a sprinkling of *kombi* drivers, secretaries, several police constables and one or two teachers. She was an excellent cook; her food was fresh, hot and wholesome and she was brisk and good-tempered. Her portions were generous. She even gave meals on credit to her more regular clients.

Business was unbelievably good, great, in fact, as long as the police did not raid her. And she could always bribe an officer or two with her servings. She knew you could rarely go wrong with the human stomach. Digging into her mouth-watering pots, fishing into her quivering blouse for change or rummaging in her capacious bag for a notebook or a pen, she was convinced that she could stave off destitution. Once a customer had remarked, 'Surely Mai George, you are now earning enough to pay five teachers every month' And she had replied, 'Ha! Ha!' (Why do people so cruelly use teaching – once a revered profession, as the yardstick for poverty.) Or, 'Come on, Mai George, you definitely only hear about "hunger" at your next doors!'

But for how long would she be safe? When would Murambatsvina, the urban 'cleansing' project, catch up with her?

***

26

At one o'clock the customers surge down to Mai George's kitchen. Lips parched and eyes ablaze with hunger. Temples sweating. Chests bristling with immodest hairs beneath exhausted industrial overalls, displaced ties; a shamelessly un-helmeted police corporal's head there, manicured secretarial feet for a sweet while released from vengeful high heels, the odd whiff of cheap perfume gone secretly stale under office desks, a pair of hopeful passers-by. Bodies pushing, calloused work hands with square thumbs thrusting out plates, humbled backs bent forward, throats bobbing, hungry fingers pointing, eyes digging and turning in the gravy, throats already slurping, swallowing ahead of their turn. With her bright apron and ladles, Mai George swivels over her pots, a benevolent matron of meals, immune to their relentless jests as each customer tries to outdo the other with *double entendre*, the unexpected and the saucy.

Mai George was a modest woman, she smiled politely when required, but she did not openly engage with her customers' repartee. Joking, like breathing, made people's lives easier. She knew this, even when she herself was not often amused. She secretly felt that humour never really worked unless the jokes were attached to specific personalities and situations.

'Honour ladies.'

'Not since they chose to go to the Beijing Conference.'

'Who says we want to be honoured? Who says we even want to be called "ladies"? Honour thy father and mother, twit.'

'Eh, eh, snotty face, get out of my way.'

'Oxygen dealer. You're bad news for the ozone layer.'

'Greedy Goriati.'

'Dinky David. Where's your sling today?'

'Knife head.'

'Scud chest.'

'Owl face.'

'*Chipendani* legs.'

'Knock knees!'

'Fanta face. Coca-Cola legs.'

'AIDS haircut.'

'Zimbo Zombie Zim.'

'*Mubvakure – kumusha kunosvikwa mai varoodzwa*. Home so far away that when you get there you'll find your mother remarried!'

'Mother who climbs trees!'

27

'No, rides order bicycles.'

'That's why you worship your ancestral spirits with Scud beer!'

'You and your gumboot dances.'

'Stinking tribalist! What about *Chembere yokwa Chivi*, that old woman from *your* village who boiled granite rocks till they were soft enough to eat?'

'But who gave you education – headmasters, nurses, army generals?'

'And who gave you standard Shona?'

'Standard 1, Standard 2, Benny and Betty, day by day. Filthy *skuz apo's*. *"Batai zvikwama vabereki!"* That's all you know. Go back to Mbare, boy.'

'Did you hear that The Dairy Company has closed down in Masvingo province, and that you will soon have to ask lactating mothers to squirt their milk into your tea?'

'Yuk! Did *you* hear there is now only one dentist left in Chitungwiza, and that *n'anga*s and *mapostori* are making a killing treating people? I'm going to join ZINATHA and become a rich herbalist.'

'Or better still, *mupostori* –

Kuti svetu kumutsetse we sugar

Kuti svetu kumutsetse we nyama'

'Don't mock other people's churches, guys. What about your *Wapusa Wapusa* sect – grabbing each other's wives as soon as they switch off the lights to "pray"?'

'Or the pastors of these rabid Pentecostals, marrying their own sisters' daughters or impregnating under-age celebrants?'

'OK. OK. Point taken, sir.'

'What's wrong with you today, Clopas? Your face is so funny it would make a skulking thief laugh.'

'What about yours? It's so ugly, children will see it in nightmares.'

'And you, my dear sir, are as horrible as a hyena.'

'Civet cat.'

'You're so poor you cook your sadza in a tea-pot.'

'And you, madam, wash your pretty face in a plate.'

'Thank you *very well*, February. You should do something about your clothes, man, all this mix and *mis*-match and layers. If a donkey came by it would munch you up mistaking you for a cabbage.'

'Fish-mouth, I'm in a hurry. Can I liberate this plate?'

'Eh, eh comrade, I thought we had long finished with this liberation business. Stay away from that plate.'

'Yes, stay away.'

'Stay away from stay-aways.'

'Off with you! You think this is sadza prepared by City Council labourers, ready in two minutes and stiff like a Shangaan staple.'

'Say, Mai George, are your chickens broilers, off-layers, good country road-runners or border jumpers?'

'Or stray *ngozi* fowls with curses strapped up to their necks which drive their slaughterers insane?'

'Shut up and eat quietly, Never. Your sandpaper belly can't tell the difference between a seasoned road-runner and an *ngozi* fowl. And besides, you are mad enough already.'

'Don't jump the queue, Petros. You didn't buy nappies for Baby Jesus.'

'Now that you've finished taking over white farms, whose bedroom are you invading tonight, comrade?'

'I'm not a comrade.'

'Or are you sleeping all night in the so-called petrol queues – tucked up in your small house's warm arms again, while some smart street kid, no, street *father*, dipsticks your wife?'

'Come on.'

'You're not a comrade? What's your real name, then? Donewell? Golden? Takesure? Toffee? Two-Boy? Obvious? Putmore? Forget? Definite?'

'Try Again!'

'No, he's not Try Again. He's Doughnut.'

'You would think this country has run out of names, sometimes. No water, no petrol, no electricity, no cooking oil, no bread, no soap and now no names.'

'Just like Zimbabwe-Rhodesia. Who was the son and who was the mother of that wretched colony?'

'And who was the grandmother?'

'*Southern* Rhodesia.'

'Reminds me of my old, half-blind granny who used to "read" the newspaper upside-down and swear, at every photograph, *"Iye Dhagirasi Smisi watinetsa zveshuwa."* Ian Douglas Smith has given us hell, for sure.'

'Oh, that goat-eyed bastard.'

'But who is not a bastard these days? At least when Goat-Eyed was in charge, we did not starve and there was a semblance of order.'

'Shut up, Bornfree. You never got expelled from school or detonated a landmine.'

'Hey guys, I know five brothers called Scud, Shoe-Shine, Shame, Anus and Progress.'

'Give us women's names too. Gender, man, Gender!'

'Is that your name, madam? Gender? Be careful how you pronounce that word in Shona.'

'Eh, eh, Christmas, watch your mouth. We have decent women here. Wives of husbands.'

'But I'm also a husband of a wife. *Ndiri murume wemunhu veduwe!*'

'Mai George is *blushing*. Look at her cheeks. My poor *ambuya*. Can we change the subject?'

'OK. Have you registered to vote, Bornfree?'

'I lost my Grade 5 school report.'

'What moron told you they need that at the registrar's office?'

'My aunt.'

'While we are at that, did you hear about the chef who said at a rally, "This time we want to win all the erections"?'

'What about the chef who never took the trouble to study the speeches his aides wrote for him and once when he reached the end, read straight on, "Sorry, chef, I have to queue for cooking oil. Now you're on your own! Good luck, sir."'

'And I bet you never heard of the venerable chief who went to America and on meeting his first African-American grabbed his hand and gasped, "Aren't you old Zebediah's mother-in-law's cousin's nephew's niece from Nembudzia?"'

'*Aiwa!* What of the two songs by our two famous musicians about old age and education which two chefs sarcastically bandied about at each other? *"Dai Ndakadzidza ... "*

"Bvuma wachembera!"

'Or, "We looked at Mai Tsvari's behind and it was OK. We looked at her front and it was OK. So we inserted her on this seat ..."'

'*Iwe. Iwe*, Bornfree, enough. We don't want you locked up. Right, Corporal Weeds?'

'It's a free country.'

'At least there is free food and accommodation in the jail.'

'Beans, salt, lice and lustful inmates. You'll come out pregnant with kwashiorkor.'

'Or stick-lean with AIDS.'

'Don't worry. With AIDS, all this diaspora business, cross-border trade and professional black people going off to wipe up old white folks' bums in London or to drive battered taxis in "Harare South", the country will soon be half empty and nobody will want for jobs or accommodation any more.'

'Only you will be paid in soap and beans and salt, like in old times. *Chikafu ndodha* – each man for himself.'

'And at the rate Murambatsvina is smashing down shacks you will lodge in dogs' kennels, with Kutu, Racer, Shumba or Boxer.'

'Out of my way, Shallot. Stop acting as if you dressed mother elephant in a bikini.'

'Eat! Eat! Eat all you can now, folks. *Idyai mughute*. Glut yourselves on Mai George's cuisine, your excellencies, highnesses, mediumnesses and lownesses, ladies and gentlemen, comrades and friends. If you could reverse evolution you would maybe develop humps like camels in which to store food for future use. By this time next year you will be munching air-pies, sipping toilet-flavoured Mukuvisi River H_2O and soaking up vitamin-rich sunshine for lunch. And you will all be stepfathers and stepmothers.'

'What's that?'

'You'll be using your legs, silly, instead of these expensive and hazardous *kombis*. Stepping off to and from work. Left, right, left, right. R1, R2.'

'Regiment 1, Regiment 2?'

'No, Renault 1, Renault 2, silly.'

'Good thing is, there will be fewer people suffering from overweight, or high blood pressure.'

'Hand over that mug, Miss Funerals. Surely I won't get AIDS from it.'

'Who's Miss Funerals?'

'You.'

'How's that?'

'Forgot how we met at Old Mambara's wake last weekend? Do you want me to tell this august assembly that you never miss a funeral? You, Madam Bowsticks, get by on funerals. Whenever you find one you announce yourself noisily, flinging yourself in the dust and howling up a storm like the appointed chief mourner. Then, eventually settling down, you wolf down a generous plate of sadza, beef and cabbage, sit back, a warm Coke in each hand, then cleaning your teeth with a matchstick, you calmly ask, "Who's died this time, folks?"'

'Ha! Ha! I'll get you. You think you're smart, don't you, Privilege? You're the guy who goes shopping but is too poor to buy anything but bones. Bones, bones, bones, every week. No offence meant to good old Chenjerai Hove, of course. A girl you've been telling grand tales about yourself sees you collecting your miserable parcel and what do you say to her in self-defence? "Er, hi, Gaudencia. What on earth are you doing, er, here? My dog has such an appetite you wouldn't, er, believe how many bones it eats every day, er, Gau!" See, Piri. You can't beat me at this.'

'What about this one? A gardener called Brown suspects his wife of having an affair with a man called Giant, whom he has never seen. On a tip from his neighbour Brown arms himself with an axe and goes to confront Giant over the matter. When he knocks on the latter's door, out comes a huge man. Thrown off guard, what does Brown say? "Sorry, sir. Scuse me, sir. *Ndiri kutengesa matemo.* I'm selling axes. Would you like to buy this sharp one, sir?"'

'We've heard that one before. Haven't we, Mai George?'

'OK, Loveness, here's a new one. Surely you'll love this. You know Privilege is a man with a little education and a modest job. He's happily married with two young children, but for eight months of the year his wife is in the rural areas, tending their little farm. Privilege of course visits her as often as he can. When his wife falls pregnant for the third time, he's thrilled. He tells his colleagues at work, "I'm going to see the children." But we all know who he's really going to "see"! Now from his rusty biology and his good SaManyika instincts, Privilege is convinced the baby grows in segments, and that with each essential coupling the baby acquires a vital new part. One weekend his bus leaves without him. Running after it, he yells "Stop, stop, driver! My baby still needs a thorax!"'

'Shame. Shame.'

'Shame. Shame. Now stop sounding like those good, little, old white "Medems".'

'Poor Piri.'

'Try again!'

'You're getting old and rueful, Biscuit. Look at your head, white as asbestos dust. Old as … who was it in the Bible? Methuselah? Are you working in a maize mill? Now that Kumbudzi Cemetery is full, have you booked yourself a grave at Greendale? Dying is getting more expensive, you know. By the shovelful. Your ghost will be pretty lonely if you choose to be buried in the rural areas, or, worse still, on the new farms. Perhaps we ought to start local ghost clubs.'

'Cremation might not be a bad idea, after all …'

'Just be sure not to snort up your father's ashes with your snuff or whatever, like that Rolling Stone fellow, what's-his-name?'

'Keith Richards.'

'Hey, guys, did you read about the Grade 7 boy who raped his own grandmother?'

'Yuk! He should be castrated at once.'

'Exit Operation Murambatsvina. Enter Operation Castration.'

'There's a new job for you, Goriati. You are manly enough. Cadet Officer, Castration Unit. Previous experience with animals a decided advantage. At least one A-level pass required. Bring your own pliers.'

'No thank you. I'm a book-keeper, man.'

'Did you hear about your cousin the economist who, on being pressed by his old grandmother to describe the nature of his work, lamely replied, *'Ah, Mbuya, basa rangu nderokunyima mari* – my job is to be stingy with money.'

'And the guy who married his own mother?'

'No need to blunt your pliers with this one, Goriati. Good luck to him with his mother-in-law, whoever and wherever she is.'

'And if they have children together how would the children address them?'

'God knows.'

'Laugh, Mai George, laugh. *Itai chikwee chaicho!* You never laugh. It's good for you, you know. It's good for your thorax. It eases the muscles of your mandibles. It tickles your little hooves. You are not the one who betrayed Jesus, you know. You didn't sign the country away with an 'X' tremulously inked in at the bottom of a piece of paper with ant-like print. You didn't invade any farm. You didn't send your husband away or starve your children. You didn't run away with the man next door …'

'And the man or woman next door is always sweet as a cold quart of Castle Lager, Spoo.'

'You mean a good, cold beer is as sweet as somebody else's husband or wife.'

'Hear, hear.'

'Laugh, sister. We can't all be chefs, you know. We're *hwakaz.*'

'*Hwakaz* of the world unite!'

'Yeah.'

'Maybe Mai George laughs in her dreams. Maybe she even dreams in full colour.'

'Leave her alone. She works very hard. She's tired.'

'If you need a new husband tell me and I'll fetch you one any time, Mai George.'

'There you go, Fambi. Waiting to pounce on innocent women with your rotten claws. Who told you every woman needs a husband?'

'Sorry, Pretty. Just jokes. But if I tried you would you say yes, Pretty?'

'Not if you were the last man left in the Mash West Province.'

'Nonsense. I already finished with you in my dreams.'

'How about this one, guys?'

'Oh, shut up, Million!'

'During one of the most prolonged ZESA load-shedding exercises a woman returned from a trip to the rural areas to find her children huddled in the dark house. "Oh my poor babies," she said with concern. "Weren't you afraid of the dark while I was away?"

"No," replied the youngest child, innocently. "We weren't afraid. But I think *baba* was scared stiff because most nights he moved in with *sisi* in the spare bedroom."'

'You haven't heard this one. A prostitute says to a prospective client, "All right, Uncle. I usually work on commission. You say you're not rich. I'll make it easy for you. I'll give you a discount. Why don't you start me off with the equivalent of a teacher's monthly salary for tonight? Half of that for short time."'

'Teachers, nurses …'

'Soldiers, too.'

'Oh, please. Give them a break.'

'And, Mai George, surely you'll like this one. A ranting, raving, Bible-thumping pastor who had made a second vocation out of stalking other men's wives had his congregation in stitches when he plucked a woman's bright red knickers out of his suit pocket and wiped his forehead with them, thinking it was his handkerchief … and announced, "I haven't finished yet …" Eh, Mai George?'

***

She had finished sweeping and tidying up her room and was dusting the headboard on which lay the photo albums of her husband and children, bound copies of her CV and job application letters, when she heard the familiar knock, rather, an insistent bang, on her door. She turned down the TV.

'Mai George! Mai George! Open up!'

She undid the bolts and threw open the door of the cottage and in stepped Mbuya MaSibanda, her landlady. The lady wore a crimson nightgown that breathed a cheap perfume and parted in the middle to expose a black petticoat silhouetting a bony frame that had seen many nights. Her hair was coiled ominously on top of her head and her cheeks were smothered with rouge. Since she'd moved in two months ago, Mai George had never seen her outside of that gown or with her hair down.

Mbuya MaSibanda planted herself on the immaculate double-bed and surveyed the neatly wallpapered room and the children's clothes, still new in their plastic wraps. 'My, my, do we have a colour TV now!'

'Yes, Mbuya,' Mai George responded, awkwardly.

'Double-bed, wardrobe, fridge, hot-plate and TV. Aren't we doing well!'

'Thank you, Mbuya.'

'There's just one slight problem with the TV, *mwanangu*. Colour. It attracts thieves, you know. And with Murambatsvina, every other man in the street is now a thief. Even the good Lord, pardon me, Jesus, would become a thief in this country. You know I have a small black and white set in the main house and all the other lodgers haven't got sets. Why didn't you tell me that you were going to buy a colour set?'

'I'm sorry, Mbuya.'

'Well, next time you buy something, let me know. Procedure, you see. That's how I run this place, how I've run this house since my husband died ten years ago, and the good Lord knows Tom Shine was a righteous man, rest his soul, though he smacked me in the face once for fawning over a stranger. And I notice you put a lock block on your door. Why would you do that with me here all day? I mean, should anything happen while you are away – say a fire or a theft – I would need access to your room. Now, *mwanangu*, aren't you going to give me a little bite to eat?'

'I eat at work and hardly bring any food at home, Mbuya.'

'Nothing at all? Not even bare bones from the bottom of your pots? From now on, bring me something to eat in the evenings. A little dish for your old landlady? I've heard about your excellent cooking, and your customers. How about a warm cup of tea and some biscuits then?'

While Mai George was switching on the kettle, Mbuya MaSibanda examined the photo album.

'This your husband and these your little babies?'

'Yes, Mbuya.'

'And you said he's been gone three years?'

'Yes, Mbuya.'

'Botswana, eh?'

'And does he send you pulas?'

'Sometimes,' she lied.

'I'll talk to you if I ever need pulas. Don't worry. He might come back or he might not. Men are funny creatures. Lecherous as goats, most of them. Just keep working for your children. Don't throw yourselves at the wolves. You said you want to go to secretarial college, don't you? Good idea. Take a leaf from my book. I've lived clean and alone for ten years, but you'll notice people gossip about me left, right and centre because my house and cottage were built with an approved plan. They know, and are jealous, that Murambatsvina can't touch me. Any men you see coming here are my children or relatives seeking help and very few of them ever put up in the house.'

Mai George poured her the tea, and as Mbuya MaSibanda munched a biscuit and took a sip, her lipstick melted into a red wound that stained the yellow mug.

'Just a few more little things, Mai George. Please don't leave your windows wide open at weekends because it finishes fresh air for the other lodgers. Disturbs the circulation, you see. And don't watch your new TV too long. It's bad for your eyes and colour TV chews up more electricity than black and white.'

Mbuya MaSibanda balanced her cup sagaciously in the saucer and went on hardly drawing breath, 'Also, you haven't been taking a turn to sweep the yard and scrub the toilet in the morning as all my lodgers should.'

'But I asked Mai Tariro next door to do my turn for me, Mbuya MaSibanda. I even pay her to do it.'

'You pay her. That's a bad precedent, *mwanangu*. It might breed the dangerous misconception that, because of money, some lodgers are free from duties and more important than others.'

'But I have to leave home at four in the morning, Mbuya MaSibanda, and you want the sweeping and scrubbing done at seven.'

'In which case you might have to leave for work after seven when it's your turn.'

Mai George stared at her TV and, as the meaning of the remark dawned on her, she snorted with half reckless abandon, 'Maybe I'd need to look for another room elsewhere.'

'Oh, you would,' Mbuya MaSibanda retorted, her eyes suddenly flickering with fire. 'You would, then? Good luck with Murambatsvina. In any case I was going to treble your rent next month. The dollar is going down and your business is booming and there are dozens of people asking for your room every week. See, child, that's the name of the game.'

'And will you get anybody to pay you that much? Will you? Or you will put in one of your "husbands"?'

Mai George glared at the older woman sitting on her bed sipping her tea. Mbuya MaSibanda seemed to age years in those seconds. Suddenly her soap and perfume took on a rank odour, like cat's urine, and her eyes blinked ashes. Her lips and hands shook and her fingers wrinkled with hate. Mai George felt like snatching the mug from her and smashing it into her teeth and only just stopped herself from doing so. Then something happened to Mai George, something that she had kept locked up for a long time escaped, her sense of the absurd. She straightened up, caught herself from drowning in the rubble of her former self. A rush of air cleared her chest and her lungs heaved. She felt her cheeks twitch and the first cackle tweaked the insides her ribs; a mere titter, a snicker, a chuckle, a chortle, swelled into a gurgle. Her sides shook uncontrollably; she giggled; then heard herself slowly explode into a guffaw. The force of her roar banged the asbestos roofing of the cottage, rattled the plates off the shelf, thrummed the rats out of the cracked walls, scuttled the spiders out of the broken floor, whooshed her papers onto the bed, tossed the mug of hot tea out of the old lady's trembling hand and hurried her out. Bravely following Mbuya MaSibanda to the door and shooing her out, almost, Mai George began to LAUGH. She laughed freely now. She laughed and laughed; she laughed at the brazen jokes that had plagued her day, at the sudden future that now glared in her face. She laughed and heard the voices of the other lodgers in the adjoining rooms shrieking with hers, conspiring with her against the ageless tyranny of the world. Her ears drowned in the echoes of her mirth as warm tears coursed down her youthful face.

A Land of Starving Millionaires

Erasmus R. Chinyani

THE MILLIONAIRE STAGGERED TOWARDS the long line of tuckshops. The stagger of an inveterate beer-drinker after one bottle too many. Only he hadn't gulped anything for quite a long time. Four days to be precise. Not even a sip of tap water, due to the unpredictable water-cuts in his part of the city. He hadn't eaten anything either, or nothing but the national staple they now call air-pie – a euphemism for one big slice of *nothing!*

Hunched under the weight of a huge plastic sack, the millionaire had the look of a man who carried the world on his back. He stopped staggering when he reached the first shop in the row and heaved the sack onto the counter. Someone once said that the only good thing about hitting your head against a brick-wall is the relief when you stop. Still, there was only a blank look on his face: the look of a punch-drunk boxer at the losing end.

'*Mudhara!* I said how much is in that bag of yours?'

'One million three hundred thousand dollars in single notes. And I want a loaf of bread and a packet of sugar.'

The shop-keeper gave a mirthless chuckle. 'Old man, don't you read the papers? Or haven't you got a radio? The prices of foodstuffs quadrupled this morning. *Half* a loaf of bread now costs one million five hundred thousand. Forget about the sugar. It's just not for your class anymore. Don't even ask how much. It will give you a heart attack. Sugar is now strictly for the super-class.'

Mr Usury Chimbadzo doubled back as if he had been dealt a swift upper-cut. He thought of his huge family. The youngest of his three wives had just given birth to – believe it or not – triplets, and his other two wives were explosively pregnant. He hadn't finished paying *roora* for the third wife and his in-laws were baying for his blood. All his school-going children had been sent home for non-payment of fees. The cumulative amount ran into *billions*. And the million in his plastic sack, which he was now being told could no longer buy half a loaf, was all he had. That, and the now useless three hundred thousand.

Back home, his children were collectively wailing like some multiple-sounding siren. All twenty-nine of them. There was a time when he was very proud of his offspring. Then, he used to boast that he was the father of not one but two 'football teams' and their match officials. He used to grin when they nicknamed him Baba vaAlphabet. That was before the *bolt-from-the-blue* arrival of the hungry triplets. Together with their older siblings, they now formed one ear-blasting choir that Baba vaAlphabet could well do without. A choral outfit made in hell. The combined sounds of their non-stop shrieks set his teeth on edge, and spun his head like some planet that had strayed wildly out of orbit. They transformed the home's once-tranquil atmosphere into one brain-exploding, funereal din.

The cacophony was such that, even if he hadn't pawned his radio, cassette player and TV to alleviate the tooth-gnashing hunger haunting his house, he could never have used them because of the collective din deafeningly produced by his children. At first their hungry cries were directed at the mothers:

'Mommy, Tadha-a! Mai, chaja-a, AMAI TIRIKUDA SADZA-A-A!!!'. The three mothers would, in frustration, either scream back at the kids, or worse, they would direct their counter-attack at the man-of-the-house, Baba vaAlphabet. But now, lately the children seemed to have taken a cue from their mothers and directed their shrill demands at the man himself – Baba vaAlphabet, the millionaire with his stash of useless dollars. And now even these had run out.

Indeed, that very morning he'd left his home – actually 'escaped' would be a more appropriate word – to, he said, 'Try and borrow money from some bank.' He'd been lying of course. The truth of the matter was that he was out to collect long-standing debts owed to him by two rascals, who happened to also be impulsive borrowers.

Although they only lived nearby, the two had been playing a cat-and-mouse game with him for a long time. In all his decades-long career as a no-nonsense money-lender, he was yet to encounter any clients as elusive as these two. So skilful were they at eluding him that he'd almost decided to give up the chase. But now, with an army of problems mustering against him, he felt he had no choice but to track them down, and wage an all-out war of his own. They'd borrowed a total of five million dollars when times were good; when a person with a *million* in his possession could rightly and proudly call himself a *millionaire* without a twinge of guilt. Now thanks to the hyper-inflationary environment threatening to submerge the nation and its once vibrant economy, times were bad for all of them.

Tough luck. The guy who had borrowed Z$3,7 million, had committed suicide, and there was a low-key funeral going on when he arrived. Judging by the low-key attendance, the low-key ceremony, and the absence of food, Mr Chimbadzo could see that it would be futile to ask any of the mourners to pay the deceased's dues. Their hungry faces told a big story. He wondered how long it would be before they joined their departed relative on his underground journey. So Chimbadzo kissed his money goodbye in an unprecedented fashion.

Jumping up and down, he yelled unprintable obscenities at the coffin as if he was addressing a living person. Yelling and hollering about the coffin's 'mother' and 'father' and their reproductive anatomy and much, *much* worse, Chimbadzo was in an uncompromising mood. A funeral is supposed to be a very sombre occasion, where respect for the dead is upheld. Under normal circumstances, any person desecrating such an occasion in the way Baba vaAlphabet was doing risked being violently upended and unceremoniously ejected. But there was something wild and menacing about the old man in their midst that froze the mourners into inaction. Something that told them to let the money-lending demon vent his fury at the motionless coffin rather than provoking him into acting it out on one of them. There was a murderous glint in his eye as he unleashed volleys of vulgar, homicidal insults, which convinced them. A person prepared to 'kill' a dead man in his coffin can be a real terror to the living.

Anyway, after Baba vaAlphabet had shouted himself hoarse, he ran out of steam, and reluctantly ambled off while stopping now and again to sneeringly take a backward look. The mourners heaved a collective sigh of relief as he went off to look for debtor Number Two. Sadly for Mr Chimbadzo, his next port of call wasn't fruitful either.

For his next debtor, a renowned pleasure-loving womaniser, who owed him one million, three hundred thousand, had long contracted the HIV virus, though he'd looked fit all along, his condition had now bloomed to full-blown AIDS. The man was on his deathbed, looking in such a bad way that even the hardened debt-collector had to calm down. One typically hot word from an enraged Chimbadzo would have seen him go out like the flame of a dying candle. For a while he just stood there, motionless, speechless before the dying man.

Then an idea struck him!

Although the place smelt of death and poverty from floor to roof, his money-lender's instinct rose to the fore and he could see how to squeeze some money from the already grieving family. Experience had taught him that distressed relatives would often be willing to do anything to save themselves from another death; trade anything in exchange for their dying relative's life – even their own souls. Old Chimbadzo made a few sympathetic noises, before saying, 'You know, Kutamburahuda here is my very best friend.' He lied, knowing the sick man was too weak to open his mouth and set the record straight. Even the dying man knew that *money* was Chimbadzo's only friend. Kutamburahuda tried to lift one of his twig-thin arms – apparently in a gesture of protest – but then his limbs slumped back on the makeshift bed. Chimbadzo continued, 'I can't let my friend die just like this. I know a man who can save his life. He's the best *n'anga* in the business. His name is … is …' he stopped to punch his head in an apparent attempt to jog his memory.

He was getting old. Lying, to him, had always come as naturally as breathing. In the past, non-existent names of non-existent people would just pop out of his mouth from nowhere. '… his name is … Dr Target Super Actelic Chirindamatura Dust. *Phew!* Now there is one hell of an *n'anga*. The best! He can cure anything, I tell you! AIDS? What AIDS? This man can cure a coffin and cause it to cough out its corpse …' He caught himself just in time '…Well, I've seen worse cases than my friend Kutamburahuda here, cured. This *n'anga* is something else I tell you! Dr Target Super Actelic Chirindamatura Dust can do anything!'

'Oh, really…!?'

'Where is this man?'

'How much does he charge per session …?'

Expectant looks brightened up the faces round the sick man's bed. Everyone knew that funerals were expensive these days.

'This man lives … well, you wouldn't know the place. He keeps his 'surgery' a closely-guarded secret. But I know, because he is my uncle … my father's father's …yes – my *uncle!* For only five million my friend here will look as fresh and healthy as a newly-born baby …' again he caught his tongue just in time. Newly-born babies are not always healthy. He thought of his perpetually screaming triplets, as if all their health lay in their wailing.

Not unexpectedly, the relatives did not have much money and could not raise the five million bucks, but they ran around and as 'luck' would have it, they managed to come up with the exact money their sick relative owed him – Z$1,3 million. They put all the money, in its various small denominations, into a plastic sack. Lifting the heavy bag to his shoulder, he purportedly headed for the great *n'anga's* surgery'.

As he left, the old debt-collector might have worn a triumphant grin after miraculously recovering his money – had times been normal. But he was only conscious of the need to buy food for his howling family. The journey home via the tuckshops and without the relief of a *kombi* was long, and the bag was heavy. Heavy, but worth it – or so he thought. Indeed had he been paid a few months previously, just over a million dollars might have solved a few of his problems.

So that's why we found him staggering towards the long row of tuckshops, a few hundred metres from his home. After the shocking news of the latest price increase, Chimbadzo stashed the hundreds and hundreds of bills back into the sack before trying the other shops. The news was not only the same, but in most instances, it was worse.

His head was whirling and spinning like a tiny scrap of paper caught in an August whirlwind. He wondered what he was going to say to his three expectant wives and battalion of children. Pre-occupied, he reached the corner of his street. Perhaps his ears had been too deafened by hunger, his mind too loaded by the sack full of poverty and his eyes too blinded by rage and despair, that he neither saw nor heard the sudden emergence of the local MP's car.

Like a fiery bat straight out of hell, the legislator's blood-red luxury Mercedes turned the corner in the typical fashion of a well-fed politician with inexhaustible amounts of fuel to burn. Baba vaAlphabet flew into the air on impact, his sack of money with him, dying long before he hit the ground. His bag burst and the dollars flew into the air, scattered like colonial propaganda pamphlets dropped from a plane. And when they did flap down to join their owner, who lay prostrate on the ground, no one rushed to pick them up.

Ashes

John Eppel

THEY COULDN'T FIND A SUITABLE URN so they used a two-litre
Lyon's Maid 'Cornish' ice-cream container. Bukhosi would have
appreciated it. That guy had a sense of humour. All his NGO friends
and a smattering of locals were there. Icrisi hugged the plastic box to
her swagging chest, Mesafi held the poem she had composed for the
occasion, Dedi carried the one-legged pigeon Bukhosi had accidental-
ly injured on his way down, head first, from the sixth floor balcony of
his uncle's apartment in downtown Bulawayo. She was going to
release it during the reading of the poem and the scattering of the
ashes. 'King' George carried the red wine and the crisps, and 'Jairos'
Jiri carried the meat – don't forget salt and pepper – and the bread
rolls. Their plan was that after the farewell ceremony at Ififi they
would have a wake, once the Parks Attendants had gone, at World's
View. They would build the fire on the mortal remains of Leander
Starr Jameson, store the food and drinks on the mortal remains of
Charles Coghlan, and consume them on the mortal remains of Cecil
John Rhodes. Bukhosi would have appreciated it. I tell you that guy
had a sense of humour, second to none.

Early on Sunday morning the chums piled into Dedi's white
Toyota 4 x 4 double cab, and Mesafi's electric blue Pajero, and they
gunned their engines for the Matopos. What a delightful squash it was:
with a frou-frou here, a frou-frou there; here a frou, there a frou,
everywhere a frou-frou. Old MacDonald (I wonder if his farm's been
designated?) would have been amazed. Past the Churchill Arms
Hotel. Past Retreat shopping centre, past the first police road block,

and – hooray – we're on the open road. Not being Rhodies, they weren't interested in the greenish hornblende and chlorite schists, which weather into a fairly fertile red clay beloved of the *Acacia karroo*; nor the yellow-billed kite on the lookout for road carnage; nor that patch of late flowering *Rhynchelytrum repens* glowing pink in the late autumn light. Honestly, the way these people appropriate the land!

The European girls in the group weren't sure, over which one of them, finally, Bukhosi had killed himself. NGOs, in the spirit of actualising social democracy, believe that if you've got something good you should share it, and they'd all, at one time or another, taken a bite out of Bukhosi. They found his dreadlocks irresistible. But these sentimental local boys, falling in love at the drop of a G-string; what's with them? That's why Icrisi was going to hang on to the ice-cream carton after Bukhosi's ashes had been scattered. You never know who might be next. Her current lover, Themba, was starting to look decidedly glum, just because of that fling with Kudakwashe. Christ, it's only a fucky-wucky!

Anyway, let's not get morbid now. Bukhosi wouldn't have wanted that. Let's do this thing. And they did it. It was beautiful to behold – except for the blasted pigeon, which refused to metamorphose into any of its symbolic components, whatever they may be. It refused even to spread its wings and soar towards heaven. Not surprising when you consider that it had been smothered in the generalised frou-frou (inclining frequently to frottage) of the journey out. The poem, with its refrain of *'super'* (pronounced zoopah), was magnificently declaimed by Mesafi, tears streaming from her eyes, and snot streaming from her nose, and spit streaming from her mouth. Women are such liquid creatures, thought 'King' George, as he felt another erection stirring. The poem went something like this (I can't remember it exactly because … well … you see … I wasn't actually there), something like:

> Bukhosi, ah, Bukhosi
> For want of a wife
> You taking (sic) your life,
> And we are sad, so sad
> Super Bhukosi.
>
> Bhukosi, ah, Bhukosi
> We giving (sic) you our 'parts'

But you wanted our hearts,
And we are sad, so sad
Super Bhukosi

Bukhosi, ah, Bhukosi
Good bye, dear friend
We missing (sic) you and your 'end',
So sad we are, so sad
Super, super, super, Bukhosi.

The scattering of the ashes from the summit of Ififi, not far from the trigonometrical beacon (ugly reminder of Rhodie appropriation) was positively transcendental. They had miscalculated – *O felix culpa* – the strength and the direction of the wind up there, and most of Bhukosi's mortal remains ended up in the hair and on the faces of the mourners. Icrisi was surprised to find that it tasted slightly salty.

After the ceremony they repaired to the picnic site, waited for the Parks officials to go home, and then appropriated the 'View of the World', consecrated ground, 'and set apart forever to be the resting place of those who have deserved well of their country'. *Quatsch!* Dragging dead grass and wood from all over the place, they built a huge fire on the grave of Leander Starr Jameson who, in death as in life, but no longer sitting, remains at the right hand of Cecil John Rhodes. The fire grew so hot that the brass lid of Jameson's grave began to blush. NGOs love building fires, the bigger and more destructive the better – perhaps because they are not allowed to build them in their own countries. Once the flames had died down and the red wine was flowing, the chums proceeded to *braai* their steaks and their chops and their *boerewors*. They hadn't realised how far away from the other grave sites (you've got to keep these Catholics at a distance) Sir Charles Coghlan's had been located, so they decided to use it as their toilet rather than a place to store the food. When the meat was ready they gathered round Rhodes' grave and used it as their dinner table.

What a feast it turned out to be! Zoopah-doopah, they declared. One toast after another was drunk to their late friend, Bukhosi, there in spirit. You could feel his presence in the scent of greasy *braai* smoke, in the texture of gritty bread rolls, in the itch between your legs. And as the night drew on, as the mourners grew a little quieter, nearly time to pack up and return to Bulawayo, to the comfort of their colonial homes, colonial boreholes, colonial swimming pools ... above all, to their colonial servants (but don't worry, we're on first-name terms), they made a unanimous decision to repeat the day's events the following weekend, at Victoria Falls. But this time – since the plastic ice-cream carton was empty – it would be a memorial service to Bukhosi, followed by a frolic in the rain forest, a booze cruise, and a gigantic *braai* on the banks of the Zambezi River.

Cocktail Hour under
the Tree of Forgetfulness

Alexandra Fuller

FOR TEN YEARS, SINCE SETTING UP THIS FISH-AND-BANANA farm in the lowveld, Mum and Dad have made their sitting room under a tree that is mostly obscured by my mother's garden, an exultant snake sanctuary of cultivated excess: creepers, buffalo grass, wild bananas, paw-paw trees, vines. It's as if here, where topsoil was brought from the plateau hundreds of miles away and where daily buckets of water were laboured up from the river, any living thing with half a desire to exist has attached itself to the ground and flourished. Snakes especially.

Then a visitor came and told Mum that the tree under which they sat was a Tree of Forgetfulness.

Mum liked the sound of that. 'Romantic,' she said, pleased. And so she sits here in her wall-free sitting room, under her ceiling of the Tree of Forgetfulness with her camp-chairs, a coffee table and her treasure of flotsam and jetsam collected on her journey through the world: a fish-shaped ashtray made by the carvers at the Kafue bridge, a bin made out of beer tops, old animal bones, snake skins, interestingly-shaped sticks, pebbles, the pod of a sausage tree, a gag novelty of a howling toy cat stuffed into a miniature sack.

Additionally, my mother has decided to associate forgetfulness with forgiveness. So she sits here every evening, under her tree, as if she were a religion. She says, 'I forget all the sins committed against me,' and she smiles in a way that she thinks makes her look beatific. 'I've forgiven all my enemies. I don't even fight with the Apostle anymore.'

Which is true, although I think this has nothing to do with the Tree of Forgetfulness, and more to do with the time. Mum grew fed up with the Apostle's tricks so she dressed up in a Halloween outfit and scared the living daylights out of the Apostle's nine children and his three wives. Mum's Halloween furnishings (bought at a jumble sale on a visit to America) came complete with a bleed-on-command Edvard Munch-inspired 'The Scream' mask, a black cloak and plastic skeleton hands. It was a lot of black nylon and white plastic. 'I nearly died of heat-stroke wearing the bally thing,' she admitted afterwards.

'What are you doing got up in that garb?' Dad asked, looking up from his *Aquaculture Today*.

'Oh nothing,' said Mum, her voice muffled by the mask.

Dad went back to his magazine.

A few days earlier someone – Mum blamed the Apostle – had made a circle of whitewash in the yard in which there were left several feathers and the depiction of an owl and several awkward stick figures representing, presumably, my mother and her many dogs. The farm's resident witch (when pressed) agreed to interpret its curse.

'This just means you and the dogs will die,' she told my mother, matter-of-factly casual.

My mother seized herself by the throat. 'Oh no!'

And when, by horrible, but not uncommon, coincidence, one of Mum's dogs was killed by a mamba some hours later she, weeping by the still body of yet another untimely-deceased Jack Russell, vowed revenge.

'All fun and games until someone loses an eye,' Dad predicted, as Mum practiced pumping blood around her plastic Edvard Munch-inspired face.

'This is not fun and games and a dog is worse than an eye,' said Mum, a sudden burp of fake blood gushing loose down the mask.

Dad chewed on his pipe placidly.

'Is there enough blood on my face, do you think?' asked Mum, for whom more is always better. She squeezed the pump frenziedly.

'Gallons,' said Dad, not looking up.

Mum marched off from the camp with resolve. Dad poured himself another cup of tea and made notes in the margin of his magazine.

***

The real Tree of Forgetfulness was in Ouidah, Benin, on the Slave

Coast. The tree itself is long-since dead and a statue of what looks like a mermaid-come-trumpeting-angel has been erected in its place. But even memorialised by this unlikely, pseudo-Nordic-looking monument, the spirit of the Tree of Forgetfulness lives on in the memory of people who visit the place every year to see where the final steps of their ancestors – the steps that carried their great-grandparents off the continent – took place.

'We turned around the tree of forgetfulness and we said goodbye to Africa,

We are going without knowing our destination; our heart is heavy with pain and our tears are bloody. The chain around our neck is so heavy!'

The Tree of Forgetfulness – around which men would walk nine times, and women seven, so that their souls would forever forget Africa – was the brainchild of the chiefs who had sold their people into slavery in the first place and who, knowing the tenacity of sorrow and revenge, did not want the torn souls of their former subjects coming back to Africa to bother them. They should have known better. There is no forgetting Africa.

***

'Whooo!' shrieked Mum, stumbling into the Apostle's family plot (she couldn't see very well. On the fifteen-minute walk down from the Tree of Forgetfulness to the Apostle's camp, the mask had fogged up and sweat was dripping into her eyes). 'Whoooo!' she yowled, and wiggled her swollen hands encased in the plastic skeleton gloves.

Upon seeing this apparition, the Apostle's family fled in horror from their disputed garden-plot of maize on the edge of my parent's banana plantation and into the underbrush (the Apostle himself was out at the time, performing his daily round of religious duties, which until that very day had included a seemingly mandatory few minutes wafting about my parents' camp in a white robe and annoying my mother and possibly – allegedly – either orchestrating or actually authoring the owl-spell magic circle and once even seizing my mother by the neck and shaking her like a rat so that she suffered whiplash and had to explain herself to the chiropractor in Lusaka).

'Whoooo!' screeched Mum, encouraged by the spectacular effect of her costume, although she was now having a hard time breathing, and she had left her asthma inhaler on the coffee table under the Tree of

Forgetfulness.

The Apostle's family stayed in the thickets, trembling, until one of the children noticed that the ghoul came accompanied by my Mum's pack of dogs and that the dogs were sniffing happily at the ghoul's feet and looking up at it expectantly as if hoping for a longer walk, or a cooling visit to the canal, or a thrown stick. 'It's always some bright child in these situations,' Mum said afterwards, as if citing facts in a historic military strategy.

'It's not a ghost,' said the child, straightening up and walking brazenly out into the open. 'It's that crazy old *mazungu* woman. Look, her dogs are with her. The dogs would not be with her if she was anybody else. She is not an *ngozi*. She is the wife of the man.' The Apostle's family re-emerged into the sunlight behind their brave child and, in forgiving humour, laughed at Mum and she laughed back at them from behind her face-dissolving mask.

Only my mother would consider this a victory over her enemies and a triumph of neighbourly love. 'Not my enemies anymore. All is forgotten,' she said. Although from that day on, the Apostle has steered clear of Mum's camp. And in return the Apostle and his ever-expanding family have been allowed to stay, unmolested by anything informed by American Halloween or Edvard Munch, on their little plot of land which they say was given to them by God and which my mother claims was given to her by the headman of the village.

'You see, I've forgotten all my enemies,' Mum says, holding out her hands as if in blessing and then counting her forgotten enemies off one by one until she runs out of fingers on both hands.

'The Tree of Wishful Thinking,' I say.

Mum gives me one of her silencing, lioness looks.

'Or Forgetfulness,' I say. After all, it's her tree.

The Mupandawana Dancing Champion

Petina Gappah

WHEN THE PRICES OF EVERYTHING went up twenty-six times in one year, M'dhara Vitalis Mukaro came out of retirement to make the coffins in which we buried our dead. And in a space of only six months, he became famous twice over, as the best coffin maker in the district and the Mupandawana Dancing Champion.

Fame is an elastic concept, especially in a place like this, where we all know the smells of each other's armpits. Mupandawana, full name Gutu-Mupandawana Growth Point, is bigger than a village but it is not yet a town. I have become convinced that the government calls Mupandawana a growth point merely to divert us from the reality of our present squalor with optimistic predictions about our booming future.

As Mupandawana is not even a townlet, a townling, or half a fraction of a town, there was much rejoicing at a recent groundbreaking ceremony for a new row of Blair toilets when the District Commissioner shared with us his vision for town status for Mupandawana by the year 2065. It is one of the biggest growth points in the country, but the only real growth is in the number of people waiting to buy coffins, and the lengthening line of youngsters waiting to board the Wabuda Wanatsa buses blasting Chimbetu songs all the way to Harare.

You will not find me joining that queue out of Mupandawana.

When the Ministry dispatched me here to teach at the local secondary, I was relieved to escape the headaches of Harare with its grasping women who will not let go until your wallet is empty and your eardrums have burst from their nagging. Mupandawana is the perfect place from which to study life, which appears to me to be no more than the punch-line to a cosmic joke played by a particularly mordant being.

So I observe life, and teach geography to schoolchildren whose only interest in my subject is knowledge of the exact distance between Mupandawana and London, Mupandawana and Johannesburg, Mupandawana and Gaborone, Mupandawana and Harare. If I cared enough, I would tell them that there is nothing there to rush for, *kumhunga hakuna ipwa*, as my late mother used to say.

But let them go, they shall find out soon enough.

Mine is not a lonely life. In those moments when solitude quarrels with me, I enjoy the company of my two friends, Jeremiah, who teaches Agriculture, and Bobojani who goes where Jeremiah goes. And then there are the Growth Pointers, as I call them, the people of Mupandawana whose lives prove my theory that life is one big jest at the expense of humanity.

Take M'dhara Vitalis.

Before he retired, he worked in a furniture factory in Harare. He had been trained in the old days, M'dhara Vitalis told us on the first occasion Jeremiah, Bobo and I drank with him. 'If the leg of one of my chairs had got you in the head *vapfanha*, you would have woken up to tell your story in heaven,' he said. 'The President sits in one of my chairs. Real oak, *vapfanha*. I made furniture from oak, teak, mahogany, cedar, ash *chaiyo*, even Oregon pine. Not these zhing-zhong products from China. They may look nice and flashy but they will crack in a minute.'

On this mention of China, Bobo made a joke about the country becoming Zhim-Zhim-Zhimbabwe because it had been sold to the Chinese. Not to be outdone, Jeremiah said 'Before the ruling party was elected, the Zimbabwe Ruins were just prehistoric rubble in Masvingo province. Now, the Zimbabwe Ruins extend to the whole country.' We laughed, keeping our voices low because the District Commissioner was seated in the corner below the window.

***

M'dhara Vitalis had looked forward to setting down the tools of his trade and retiring to answer the call of the land. 'You don't know how lucky you are,' he was often heard to say to the fellows who idled around Mupandawana. 'You have no jobs so you can plough your fields.'

He had spent so much time in Harare that he appeared not to see that the rows to be ploughed were stony; when the rains came, there was no seed, and when there was seed, there were no rains. Even those like Jeremiah, who liked farming so much, that they had swallowed books all the way to the agricultural college at Chibhero, had turned their backs on the land, in Jeremiah's case, by choosing to teach the theory of farming to children who, given even an eighth of a chance, would sooner choose the lowliest messenger jobs in the cities than a life of till, till, tilling the land.

M'dhara Vitalis was forced to retire three years earlier than anticipated. His employer told him that the company was shutting down because they could not afford the foreign currency. There would not be money for a pension, he was told, the money had been invested in a bank whose directors had run off with it *kwazvakarehwa* to England. He had been allowed to keep his overalls, and had been given some of the tools that he had used in the factory. And because the owner was also closing down another factory, one that manufactured shoes, M'dhara Vitalis and all the other employees were each given three pairs of shoes.

Jeremiah, Bobo and I saw him as he got off the Wabuda Wanatsa bus from Harare. 'Thirty years, *vakomana*,' he said to us, as he shook his head. 'You work thirty years for one company and this is what you get. *Shuwa, shuwa,* pension *yebhutsu*. Heh? Shoes, instead of a pension. Shoes. These, these ...'

The words caught in his throat.

'*Ende futi dzinoshinya*, all the pairs are half a size too small for me,' he added when he had recovered his voice. We commiserated with him as best we could. We poured out all the feeling contained in our hearts.

'Sorry, M'dhara,' I said.

'Rough, M'dhara,' said Jeremiah.

'Tight,' said Bobojani.

We watched him walk off carefully in his snug-fitting shoes, the plastic bag with the other two pairs dangling from his left hand.

'Pension *yebhutsu*,' Jeremiah said, and, even as we pitied him, we laughed until tears ran down Jeremiah's cheeks and we had to pick Bobojani off the ground.

For all that he did not have a real pension, M'dhara Vitalis was happy to retire. Some three kilometres from the growth point was the homestead that he had built with money earned from the factory, with three fields for shifting cultivation. Between them, he and his wife managed well enough, somehow making do until the drought came in two consecutive years and inflation zoomed and soared and spun the roof off the country. M'dhara Vitalis went back to Harare to look for another job, but who wanted an old man like him when there were millions unemployed? He looked around Mupandawana and was fortunate to find work making coffins. M'dhara Vitalis was so efficient that he made a small contribution to the country's rising unemployment – his employer found it convenient to fire two other carpenters. And that was how he became known as the coffin maker with the nimblest fingers this side of the Great Dyke.

***

We had seen his hands at work, but of his nimble feet, we had only heard. And as the person who told us of his acrobatics on the dance floors of Harare was the man himself, there was reason to believe that he spoke as one who ululated in his own praise. As Jeremiah said, 'There is too much seasoning in M'dhara Vita's stories.'

All his exploits seemed to have taken place in the full glare of the public light. 'I danced at Copacabana, Job's Night Spot, and the Aquatic Complex. There is one night I will never forget when I danced at Mushandirapamwe and the floor cleared of dancers. All that people could do was to stand and watch. *Vakamira ho-o,*' he told us. We laughed into our beers, Jeremiah, Bobojani and I, but we laughed too much and we laughed too soon. We soon came to see that the trumpet he blew in his own praise was, if anything, of an unduly low volume.

M'dhara Vita's employer was the Member of Parliament for our area. As befitting such a man of the people, the Honourable had a stake in the two most thriving enterprises in the growth point, so that the profits from Kurwiragono Investments t/a No Matter Funeral Parlour and Coffin Suppliers accumulated interest in the same bank account as those from Kurwiragono Investments t/a Why Leave Guesthouse and Disco-Bar. And being one on whom fortune had smiled, our Honourable could naturally not confine his prosperous seed to only one woman. Why Leave was managed by Felicitas, the

Honourable's fourth wife, a generous sort who had done her bit to make a good number of men happy before she settled into relative domesticity with the Honourable. As one of those happy men, I retained very fond memories of her, and often stepped into the guest-house for a drink and to pass the time. She always had an eye out for the next chance, Felicitas, which is how she came to replace me with the Honourable, and she decided that what the bar needed was a danc-ing competition.

The first I heard of it was not from Felicitas herself, but when I saw groups of dust-covered schoolchildren at break-time dancing the *kon-gonya*. Now, the sexually suggestive *kongonya* is the dance of choice at ruling party gatherings, so that I thought only that they must be prac-tising for a visit from yet another dignitary. Later that evening as I passed the guesthouse, I saw another crowd of children dancing the *kongonya*, while another pointed to the wall of the building. Curious at this seemingly random outbreak of *kongonya* in the youth of Mupandawana, I approached the guesthouse. The youngsters scat-tered on my approach, and I saw that they had been admiring a poster on which was portrayed the silhouette outline of a couple captured in mid-dance. The man's back was bent so far that his head almost touched the ground, while his female partner, of a voluptuousness that put me in mind of Felicitas, had her hands on her knees with her bot-tom almost touching the ground.

Below this enraptured couple were the words:

Why Leave Guesthouse and Disco-Bar
in association with
Mupandawana District Development Council
is proud to present the search for the:

Mupandawana
Dancing
Champion.

Join us for a night of celebration and dancing!
One Night Only!!

There followed details of the competition to be held a fortnight from then, and the main prizes to be won, the chief of which was one drink on the house once a week for three months.

Mupandawana is a place of few new public pleasures. In the next two weeks, the excitement reached a pitch that escalated on the night itself. In Why Leave assembled Mupandawana's highest and lowest. In their cheap and cheerful clothes they congregated in the main room of the guesthouse and poured out into the night: the lone doctor doing penance at the district hospital, the nurses, the teachers, the security guards, the storekeeper from Chawawanaidyanehama Cash and Carry and his two giggling girl assistants, the District Commissioner in all his frowning majesty, the policemen from the camp, some random soldiers, the people from the nearby and outlying villages. You could have carved out the excitement with a knife, distributed a generous chunk to everyone in Mupandawana and the growth points beyond, and you still would have had plenty to spare.

Tapping feet and impatient twitches and shakes showed that the people were itching to get started, and when Felicitas turned on the music, they needed no further encouragement. The music thumped into the room, the Bhundu Boys, Alick Macheso and the Orchestra Mberikwazvo, Andy Brown and Storm, System Tazvida and the Chazezesa Challengers, Cephas 'Mwotomuzhinji' Mashakada and Muddy Face, Hosiah Chipanga and Broadway Sounds, Mai Charamba and the Fishers of Men, Simon 'Chopper' Chimbetu and the Orchestra Dendera Kings, Tongai 'Dehwa' Moyo and Utakataka Express, and, as no occasion could be complete without him, Oliver 'Tuku' Mtukudzi and the Black Spirits. They sang out their celebratory anthems of life gone right; they sang out their woeful, but still danceable, laments of things gone wrong. And to all these danced the Growth Pointers, policeman and teacher, nurse and villager, man and woman, young and old. There was *kongonya*, more *kongonya*, and naturally more *kongonya* – ruling party supporters in Mupandawana are spread as thickly as the rust on the ancient Peugeot 504 that the Honourable's son crashed and abandoned at Sadza Growth Point. Bobojani was in there with the best of them, shuffling a foot away from the District Commissioner, while Jeremiah and I watched the activities from the bar.

The Growth Pointers did themselves proud, and then some. The security guard who stood watch outside the Building Society danced the Borrowdale even better than Alick Macheso, its inventor. Dzinganisayi, widely considered to be the Secretary-General of the Mupandawana branch of ZATO (*aka* the Zimbabwe Association of

Thieves' Organisations) proved to be as talented on the dance floor as he was reputed to be in making both attended and unattended objects vanish. Nyengeterayi, the gigglier of the girl assistants from Chawawanaidyanehama Cash and Carry got down on hands and knees and improvised a dance that endangered her fingers, given the stomping eagerness of the dancing feet around her.

And who knew that the new Fashion and Fabrics teacher could move her hips like that? As I watched her gyrate to Tuku, a stirring arose in my loins, and I began to reconsider the benefits of long-term companionship.

Then, out of the corner of my eye, I saw M'dhara Vita enter.

He was dressed in a suit that declared its vintage as circa 1970s. The trouser legs were flared, while the beltline that must have once hugged his hips and waist was rolled up and tied around his waistline with an old tie. The jacket had two vents at the back. He wore a bright green shirt with the collar covering that of his jacket. On his head was a hat of the kind worn by men of his age, but his was set at a rakish angle, almost covering one eye. And on his feet were one third of his pension.

'*Ko*, Michael Jackson*ka*,' Jeremiah said as we nudged each other.

M'dhara Vitalis gave us a casual nod as, showing no signs of discomfort in the general foot area, he walked, almost pranced, to the dance floor.

And then he danced.

The security guard's Borrowdale became an Mbaresdale. Dzinganisayi's movements proved to be those of a rank amateur. Nyengeterayi's innovations were revealed to be no more than the shallow ambitions of callow youth. M'dhara Vitalis danced them off the floor to the sidelines where they stood to watch with the rest of us. He knew all the latest dances, and those before the latest. We gaped at his reebok and his water pump. He stunned us with his running man. He killed us with his robot. And his snake dance and his break dance made us stand and say ho-o. His moonwalk would have made Michael himself stand and say ho-o. The floor cleared, and only he and the Fashion and Fabrics teacher were left.

M'dhara Vitalis was here. The teacher was there.

The teacher was here. M'dhara Vitalis was there.

M'dhara Vitalis moved his hips. The teacher moved her waist.

M'dhara Vitalis moved his neck and head.

The teacher did a complicated twirl with her arms.

M'dhara Vitalis did some fancy footwork, *mapantsula* style.

The teacher lifted her right leg off the ground and shook her right buttock.

And then Felicitas put on Chamunorwa Nebeta and the Glare Express. As the first strains of 'Tambai Mese Mujairirane' filled the room, we saw M'dhara Vitalis transformed. He wriggled his hips. He closed his eyes and whistled. He turned his back to us and used the vent in the back of the jacket to expose his bottom as he said *'Pesu, pesu,'* moving the jacket first to one side and then to the other. 'Watch that waist,' I said to Jeremiah.

'If only I was a woman,' said Jeremiah.

That last dance sealed it, the Fashion and Fabrics teacher conceded the floor. By popular acclaim, M'dhara Vita was crowned Mupandawana Dancing Champion. It was a night that Mupandawana would not forget.

***

This was just as well because the one-night-only threat of the poster came true in a way that Felicitas had not anticipated. Two days after M'dhara Vita's triumph, the governor of our province summoned our Honourable MP to his office in Masvingo. A bright young spark, one of the countless army of men who, in the words of my favourite writer, are paid to get offended on behalf of the ruling party, had taken a careful look at the poster and noticed that the first letters of the words Mupandawana Dancing Champion spelled out the acronym of the unmentionable opposition party. Naturally, this had to be conveyed to the appropriate channels.

'What business does a ruling party MP have in promoting the opposition, the puppets, those led by tea-boys, the detractors who do not understand that the land is the economy and the economy is the land and that the country will never be a colony again, those who seek to reverse the consolidation of the gains of our liberation struggle,' so said the governor, shaking with rage. I only knew that he shook with rage because Felicitas said he did, and she only knew because the Honourable told her so.

The upshot of this was that there were no more dance competitions, and M'dhara Vita, the coffin maker, remained the undefeated dancing champion of our growth point. He took his a one-drink-a-week prize for what it was worth, insisting on a half bottle of undiluted Chateau brandy every Friday evening. 'Why can't he drink

Chibuku like a normal man his age?' Felicitas asked, with rather bad grace, to which I responded that if he had been a normal man of his age, he would not have been the dancer he was.

To appreciate his dexterity is to understand that he was an old man. They had no birth certificates in the days when he was born, or at least none for people born in the rural areas, so that when he trained as a carpenter at Bondolfi and needed a pass to work in the towns, his mother had estimated his age by trying to recall how old he was when the mission school four kilometres from his village had been built. As befitting one who followed in the professional footsteps of the world's most famous carpenter, he had chosen 25 December as his birthday, so that his age was a random selection and he could well have been older than his official years. What was beyond dispute was that he danced in defiance of the wrinkles around his eyes.

Even if he had not gotten his drinks on the house, many of us would have bought him, if not his favourite brandy, then a less expensive alternative. There were no competitions and no more posters, but we began to gather at the guesthouse every Friday evening to watch M'dhara Vita. Fuelled by the bottom-of-the-barrel brandy and the *museve* music, his gymnastics added colour to our grey Fridays.

And it was no different on that last Friday.

'Boys, boys,' he said as he approached the bar where I stood with Bobojani, Jeremiah and a group of other drinkers.

'*Ndeipi* M'dhara,' Jeremiah greeted him in the casual way that we talked to him; none of that respect-for-the-elders routine with M'dhara Vita. He cracked a joke at our expense, and we gave it right back to him, he knocked back his drink, and proceeded to the dance floor. Felicitas had learned that it was the Congolese rumba that demanded agile waists and rubber legs that really got him moving. Thus on that night, the Lubumbashi Stars blasted out of the stereo as M'dhara Vitalis took centre stage. He stood a while, as though to let the brandy and the music move its way though his ears and mouth to his brain and pelvis. Then he ground his hips in time to the rumba, all the while his eyes closed, and his arms stretched out in front of him.

'*Ichi chimudhara chirambakusakara,*' whistled Jeremiah, echoing the generally-held view that M'dhara Vitalis was in possession of a secret elixir of youth.

'I am Vitalis, shortcut *Vita, ilizwo lami ngi*Vitalis, danger *basopo. Waya waya waya waya!*' He got down to the ground, rolled and shook.

We crowded around him, relishing this new dance that we had not seen before. What was amazing was that he had not even had a second drink before trying it.

He twitched to the right, and to the left. The music was loud as we egged him on. He convulsed in response to our cheering. His face shone, and he looked to us as if to say, 'Clap harder.'

And we did.

It was only when the song ended and we gave him a rousing ovation and still he did not get up that we realised that he would never get up, and that he had not been dancing, but dying.

***

As M'dhara Vitalis left Why Leave feet first, it was left to Bobojani, with his usual eloquence, to provide a fitting commentary on the evening's unexpected event.

'Tight,' he said.

There was not much to add after that.

We buried him in one of the last coffins he ever made. I don't know whether he would have appreciated that particular irony. I am sure though, that he would have appreciated making the front page of the one and only national daily newspaper.

The story of his death appeared on the front page, right under the daily picture of the President. If you folded the newspaper three quarters of the way to hide the story in which was made the sunny prediction that inflation was set to go down to 2757% by the year- end, all you saw was the story about M'dhara Vita. They wrote his name as Fidelis instead of Vitalis, and called him a pensioner when he hadn't got one; unless, of course, you counted those three pairs of shoes.

Still, the headline was correct.

'Man dances self to death.'

That, after all, is just what he did.

Reckless

Albert Gumbo

PENGA WALKS IN TO FINE FARE'S OFFICE. It is a large office with one side of the wall dominated by a large window that gives Fine Fare a bird's eye view of the yard from the first floor. His eyesight is legendary and he's been known to spot a driver unwrapping a chocolate packet in his cab five trucks away. When this happens, Fine Fare simply grabs his walkie-talkie and bellows into it: '005, no eating in the damn cab!' Despite his nickname, Fine Fare abhors the idea that anyone should eat in his trucks and will suspend drivers whose cabs are found with food crumbs in them during impromptu health and hygiene inspections. The opposite wall is covered with a vast map of Southern Africa. It is dotted with green pins depicting the whereabouts of Everywhere Anytime Trucking (EAT) vehicles. There is a red pin stuck on the N1 highway to Zimbabwe just before Polokwane. That means a truck has broken down. Fine Fare looks up, wafer with cheese atop in hand, and motions to Penga to sit down as he finishes a mouthful of several wafers with a sip of the goat's milk that always sits in a glass on his desk. He chews with his mouth open and Penga cannot help but notice the cement mixer at work.

Fine Fare has earned his nickname from the staff not only because of his huge appetite and snacking habits but also because he likes to believe that he only eats the finest foods. He likes to remind his staff that he will only eat the best of what he likes. When he orders fish and chips for instance, the messenger knows that he can only buy the chips from Chippies of Chisipite, and the fish from Fish Angler of Avondale. The poor man rides twenty kilometers just to bring lunch to Fine Fare's office in Graniteside and the menu changes every day.

'What's a little motor cycle fuel for a quality life, neh?' Fine Fare always asks when his book-keeping wife complains about expenses. 'Just keep the debt collection on track,' he likes to add. 'You're doing a good job with that idiot at Fresh Harvest. Stay on top of him.' His wife always responds with a smile and sets off on her twice weekly debt collection rounds, always heading for Fresh Harvest first. The assistant book-keeper smiles knowingly. She hates Fine Fare for the way he treats his wife and is only too happy to protect the secret that they both share. The owner of Fresh Harvest gives her a monthly pack of fruit, vegetables and imported fruit juice to ignore the fact that Fine Fare's wife does a lot more than debt collection on the leather settee in his private office. What's a little dark secret for a huge pack of healthy food for her little boy, Donnell?

Fine Fare wipes his mouth daintily with a blue serviette. He has five colours of serviettes and his secretary is under strict instructions to bring out the one that most closely matches whatever shirt he is wearing. After another sip of milk he asks: 'Is your visa still valid?'

'Yes boss,' Penga replies.

'Good. 007 is down just outside Polokwane. It is Vila again,' he adds, mentioning the name of the driver who has the highest rate of breakdowns per 100,000 km.

Penga sighs, 'He's certainly not in the running for driver of the year.' He wonders why the worst performing driver has been allowed to drive the refrigerated truck.

'Leave right away. Take the Fortuner. We do not want to run the risk of the product going bad or that idiot at Fresh Harvest will not pay in full.'

***

Before departing, Penga asks the Personnel Officer to have someone put his allocation of sugar into the Toyota Fortuner so that he can leave it at home when he collects his travel bag. Their company transports sugar for the sugar company, thus an associated perk is that the marketing team always get product when it is in short supply. Fine Fare prides himself on the fact that he looks after the welfare of his staff, often allocating them flour, sugar and cooking oil – products that are scarce in the country but available to him – because his company is the transport service provider for many a manufacturer. The staff pay the retail price, of course, but then they would not be able to get it if they worked elsewhere.

Fifteen minutes later, Penga arrives at Barberton Police Station to clear the Fortuner for cross-border travel. There are about ten cars ahead of him on the gravel parking lot and he waits patiently as they inch towards the first check-point. There, an officer checks his engine and chassis numbers after casting a somewhat disdainful look at Penga who does not look like somebody who should be driving a Toyota Fortuner. The next bit involves going to queue outside Office 4 where a lady officer in civilian clothes stamps the piece of paper given him at the first check. The reason for the elaborate checks is the car-theft ring in Southern Africa that stretches from Cape Town to Kinshasa. At the third office, after a further fifteen minutes in the queue, Penga is confronted by a surreal scene. The lady officer is gorging herself on Maputi, a popular form of bloated popcorn, and asking him questions with her mouth full. He can see the popcorn dancing around her tonsils as she asks for this letter then the other. A young male officer walks in and announces that he's walking to the shops nearby, if she wants anything. She tells him to bring her a cream soda. Reaching into her bra, she pulls out a few tired-looking notes and thrusts them into his open hand sighing heavily, muttering about the cost of things and wondering aloud when the 'breetish will stop sabotaging our economy'. A moment later, Penga emerges from her office to go and queue in front of the last check-point. As he waits, he watches three brand-new cars arriving in the first queue. They're all being driven by Chinese men. The people in the queue stare enviously and exchange some xenophobic pleasantries that help them feel better about not driving such smart cars. Finally Penga can leave the police station and after speeding home and grabbing his bag which he throws onto the back seat, he heads for the highway and is met with rank chaos.

Someone is chasing the goat sellers who ply their trade where the highway to Beitbridge begins. As the sellers scatter to save themselves, their goats, used to following their masters, follow suit and there is pandemonium as buses, trucks and passenger vehicles swerve to avoid them. After the police have confiscated the goats as evidence for use in court cases, the traffic jam lasts twenty minutes. Tempers fly over who should reverse first to clear the road. As he inches past the Granville Cemetery where three of his relatives lie, all as a result of AIDS, Penga is already an hour behind schedule and he 'puts foot' as soon as the road is clear. Within a few minutes, he is cruising at 160 kilometres per hour on the carpet to Masvingo as the highway is known. At a straight stretch in the road, he ejects Fine Fare's Kylie Minogue CD and replaces it with the Sista Bettina one which is the current rage. Just as he looks back up to the road, he swears softly to himself and hits the brakes. Too late! The cop standing in the middle of the road pointing a hair dryer at him is already grinning broadly. He indicates to the side of the road and Penga knows he's fucked. The traffic cop saunters over.

'Younger man, you want to kill yourself?'

'No, Officer,' replies Penga with a contrite look. He has already decided to call the man 'officer' hoping the respectful title will earn him a few points on the forgiveness scale.

'But you were doing 159.4 kilometres per hour!'

'Sorry, but I'm rushing to Polokwane. Our truck has broken down.'

The officer looks at him with pity and the lecture starts.

'Younger man, I've been a traffic officer for fifteen years and I can assure you that when you are in a hurry, you almost never get there. Slow but steady keeps you and others alive. Is this your car?'

'No Officer. It belongs to my boss.'

'Let me see your license and papers.'

Penga sighs as he reaches for the cubby hole. He's about to go through the Baberton police station story again.

'Oh, am I delaying you younger man?'

'No, no, Officer. Not at all. You're just doing your job.'

'You'd better know that. My grandfather was a policeman. In fact, there's a street named after him in Zambia, then Northern Rhodesia. He was on first name terms with Sir Roy Welensky. Do you know who that was?' Without waiting for a response, the elderly cop continues. 'Then my father also became a policeman. He retired as officer in charge of Sun Yet Sen police station and that, young man, is an honour. I am the first traffic officer in the family and I always get my man. I have the highest record of traffic fines in the whole country.'

'Congratulations, Officer,' said Penga as he handed over his papers and regretted it immediately.

'Are you being sarcastic younger man?'

'No, Officer, I think it's a very good record.'

'You younger people try to be too clever by half.' He walks round to the front of the car to confirm its registration number and spots something missing on the windscreen.

'Where is your zet tee vee license?' He exclaims in a tone that suggests that Penga has committed blasphemy.

Penga groans inwardly. Fine Fare does not have that sort of thing on any of his cars because he loves to declare to all and sundry that he only watches DSTV. Penga apologises profusely saying his boss had only just bought the car, and then this emergency came up. Penga promises with a sincere look to have that rectified as soon as he returns.

'Well young man, first speeding, and then no zet tee vee license because your boss likes watching imperialist propaganda. So what do we do now?'

'I don't know, Officer. I'm sorry. What do we do?'

'You make a suggestion, younger man. You drive fast but your brain moves slowly.'

'How about a contribution to the retirement fund for distinguished traffic officers?'

'Excellent suggestion, but the receipt book is back at HQ.'

Penga smiles and there's an understanding. Soon he's speeding down the highway again. He does not need to stop for refueling because the Toyota goes on and on and the gauge appears happy to stay where it is for periods on end even with the air-con on.

At the border, Penga breezes through immigration getting his passport stamped quickly, clears customs and then goes off to look for the Interpol officer for his car clearance. The officer looks through his papers, stamps them and Penga walks out of the building happy with himself. At the exit, a man in civilian clothing asks for his stamped papers and asks a few questions.

'How much do you have in Zimbabwe dollars?'

The lie comes easily. ' Only Z$150,000 for lunch on my way back.'

The man does not seem to care what he uses it for. 'And forex?'

Penga hesitates ever so slightly and the plain-clothes man frowns. Fine Fare has given him hard currency in case there is a need to buy spares. The money is safely ensconced in the box of tissue lying casually on the dashboard. It is such an audacious place that Fine Fare reckons the cops would never look there. Penga consciously avoids looking at the box. He reaches for his wallet and makes a pretense of counting silently to himself, 'SAR375'.

'You know the ara bee zed regulations on foreign currency?'

'Well sort of. ... I think the governor said we're allowed

more than SAR375.'

'What else do you have?'

'That is all.'

The officer asks him to open the boot and at that moment Penga lets out an involuntary gasp. He's just remembered his sugar allocation.

'What is thees? Are you smuggling sugar? Do you know *that* is an offence?

'No, Officer. It is for my own use.'

'For your own use in South Africa!'

'No, for home. I was in a hurry and I forgot to drop it at the house. I swear I am not smuggling.'

'Well, you will have to leave it here. I will give you a seizure notice. Park over there. You're blocking the rest of the traffic.'

Penga's heart sank again. He was not having the best of days.

'Do you have any export permit for this sugar?'

'Officer, please, it is only 10 kgs! How can I smuggle sugar to a country where there is plenty of it? We can phone my company. This is my allocation and I left in a hurry. I am just going to fix one of our trucks which has broken down.'

'Which company?'

'EAT'

'Oh, why didn't you say so? Your drivers bring me groceries from time to time. Do you know Vila?'

'That's the one who has broken down.'

'Oh shame, carry on and tell him to hurry up with my cellphone. So that's why he's late. I was expecting him yesterday afternoon.'

Penga smiles at life in Zimbabwe as he is waved through. It is not what you know; it is who you know and what you have to offer that determines your success in the new economy.

A few hours later he's approaching the first flyover after Polokwane on the highway looking for an off-ramp. He spots the bright orange colour of the EAT truck as he gets back on the N1 to Zimbabwe. Vila is happy to see him after their conversation half an hour before. They quickly replace the defective part and Penga follows slowly behind Vila until the border post. He leaves him there, knowing he'll be there for a full day clearing customs, and decides to take the Bulawayo route back to Harare. He doesn't always get to drive a Toyota Fortuner, after all. He nearly writes it off after narrowly avoiding a herd of goats between Beitbridge and Gwanda but in a matter of hours he is arriving in Bulawayo and heading to the The Brass Monkey for a drink.

It's a fantastic setting and he wonders aloud to no one in particular why there is no one else in the bar at 8 p.m.

'Bulawayo people live in barracks. At 6 p.m. they're all indoors waiting for tomorrow,' says the barman. 'They don't like going out.' Penga orders a Jack Daniels. He saw the ad on DSTV once at Fine Fare's house. They don't have any. He asks for a Johnny Walker black label. They don't have any either so he settles for any whisky. A man with his partner snorts and says something in a language that Penga doesn't understand. His companion laughs softly. Penga looks up, guessing that the remark is aimed at him. The man is ugly but he has a beautiful woman by his side. He is fat and two lines mark his face where the cheeks fold downwards towards his chin. His nose looks like his maker planted it as an afterthought. Ignoring the man and looking at his partner he retorts:

'Shit you're ugly.'

The beast of a man frowns. 'Sorry?'

'I've never seen anyone as ugly as you.'

The beast looks around as if to seek confirmation that someone else has heard what he has just heard. He gets off his bar stool and leans forward like a person who is hard of hearing, 'Do you want to repeat what you just said?' he says very slowly.

'Isn't there a law against being so ugly?'

The man starts walking towards him as the barman wonders why this young man with the heavy accent from the north wants to have his balls cut off. He swiftly makes his way round the other side of the bar and intervenes while signaling to the bouncers at the door.

'There's no fighting allowed here,' he murmurs in a soft but decidedly firm voice. The beast lifts a finger in Penga's direction.

'Be careful young man. Be very careful.'

Penga smiles at the beast and his lovely companion. He grew up in Mufakose and has been in a scrap or two. He finishes his whisky and saunters past the couple winking at the girl as he walks by. The beast reaches for him but he ducks quickly, laughs aloud and skips out of the club. He jumps into the car and speeds off towards the Holiday Inn. Trying to look important, he checks in, orders room service from the Spur and goes upstairs.

The next day, he drives to an address in the Avenues given to him by Vila for fuel. He can't believe that fuel is sold in the parking lot of a block of flats.

'Isn't it dangerous?' he asks rather naively.

'What do you want us to do? Put it through a cow?' responds the supplier. The others roar with laughter and Penga decides not to debate the matter. After negotiating a price he fills his tank at the black market rate and waits for Vila to arrive in Bulawayo where he's scheduled to drop part of his load at a wholesalers company in Falcon Street. Satisfied that all is well, he leaves Bulawayo just after lunch and arrives back in Harare three hours later, just in time to hand back the car to Fine Fare who is still at his desk, eating.

'My sugar was confiscated at the border.'

Fine Fare roars with laughter showing a mixture of crushed grapes in his mouth.

'Why did you take it with you?' he chuckles. 'I'll see to it that you get an extra allocation tomorrow. Now go home and rest. Leave the keys on my desk.'

As he walks to the bus stop to go home, Penga's workmates ask why he is not taking his new car home. He smiles to himself. Nothing has changed in the two days he has been away. Zimbabwe, petty all round.

Specialisation

Lawrence Hoba

One man straightens the wire, another puts the head while another sharpens the tip. In this way all men make more pins than they would if each was to make the whole pin. Adam Smith

SUDDENLY, EVERYTHING SEEMED TO have gone wrong; but no one could tell what the cause was nor what had really happened. We sat down – Chimoto, Baba Nina and I – and in hushed tones discussed what might have occurred. But exactly five hours and two gallons of thick home-brewed opaque beer later, we'd only succeeded in getting ourselves numbly drunk and raising our voices to height-of-hot-summer cicada highs. We could have gone on. But Mama Nina came into the study crying and saying that she couldn't stand men that knew how to do nothing except drink and argue. Why didn't we ever think of consulting the spirit medium, after all?

It was hot and a Saturday when we all crammed into the 4 x 4 single-cab truck that we had taken over along with the farm and all the other equipment. We could have gone on a Sunday, but I'd said that I would never dare insult God. Baba Nina had been the white man's driver and he still drove the truck, though I was unsure of whether it was for himself, Chimoto or me. Baba Nina had grasped specialisation with gusto and had undertaken to master the art himself. Every morning he woke up to the sound of the first singing bird. He washed the car spotlessly clean, and checked the oil and the fuel gauge. By kicking each tyre with his booted feet, he could tell which one needed more pressure, so that he could take the pump and do just that. His ritual took him until about tea-time, though tea was now rather scarce

69

because of the countrywide sugar shortages.

Afterwards, he checked on the tractors, all three of them. He cursed and ranted every time Chimoto brought back a tractor covered in dust, mud and grime. 'Can't you even plough without muddying her up? Look at yourself,' Baba Nina would size Chimoto up and down, 'you're as dirty as the plough itself. You even leave mud on the seat!' He would pause and then turn to me. 'How can specialisation ever work if we keep frustrating each other's efforts? I'm a driver, a vehicle engineer, not a cleaner!'

I'd decided to sit next to the window where the rushing wind would cool my face and I could gaze at the vast expanses of repossessed land without straining my neck. Here and there fences that once restricted wild animals and cattle from moving onto the tarred road lay rotting on the ground or had been completely removed. It had been a rush, just like the gold rush. Everyone had wanted to take the closest entry into and onto the farms to grab the juiciest piece of ancestral soil they could find. No one had thought about tomorrow, life after the rush. The hunger had been too great and finding gates was just a waste of time.

Everywhere the land now lay bare and black, the skeletons of charred trees standing where forests had not yet been cleared. Almost everyone burnt the grass when they thought they had seen the first signs of rain. Traditional habits die hard, even when you haven't tilled for a century. The whole countryside had caught fire but no rain had followed. Not then; not now. But we could never be charged with destroying the forests with fire – it was a cultural practice. And there had always been grass-burning even before we took over the farms. It was only that now nature had decided to show us her harsher side and, of course, we had not had time to repair the fireguards, a colonial institution.

'Stop here, Chimoto,' commanded Baba Nina. We had passed the turn-off to the main road. The spirit medium's hut stood alone in the mountains, on a plateau where mermaids were said to be heard singing each morning at a spring well. Baba Nina braked hard, reversed and got onto the faint track. He manoeuvred the truck among the stones and burnt tree stumps. This way we could only take the car as far as the foot of the mountain. We got out and trudged towards the hidden hut. I felt tired and thirsty from the heat, and looking at Chimoto and Baba Nina, I knew they felt the same. 'Do you think we will find the spring with water in this drought?' I asked, breaking the silence that enveloped us.

'Shh,' Chimoto and Baba Nina said at the same time. I kept quiet, not wanting to ask why I had to shut up. Each of us walked differently. It was our specialisation. Walking. Most people said that I wobbled lazily. They said it was because of the books I'd taken to swallowing since an early age. Baba Nina walked with short brisk steps. But Chimoto had an air about him. He walked with the gaiety of all those who have ever fought in a war, whether in defeat or in victory. One need not search far for people of Chimoto's walking specialisation. They prided themselves as the country's liberators, though during the guerilla war they'd been called terrorists by Ian Smith's government or *vanamukoma* by the fearful majority in the barren sandy reserves.

And as a relic of the war, just as some wear the *légion d'honneur* or other war memorablia, Chimoto carried a limp in the left leg where he said a bullet had entered but not come out. The limp, however, only became visible to those who didn't know him when he was angry, which was often, and when they were at a meeting for the war veterans. There was money from government for those who were injured during the struggle. It was he, Chimoto, after one of their so many meetings about this or that money who had come to tell us how absurd he thought it was that twenty years after independence, we still had not got that for which we had shed our blood.

So all we had needed to do was to wait for Baas Kisi to go to the city, as he always did every Friday, and then telephone him and say, 'You white kaffir, don't bother showing your nigger farse here because we will do your ace meat meat with a shap panga. The farm and everything on it is now ours. We, the soverin sons of the soil.' Chimoto had written down the statement so that I would not forget a word he wanted said. I told him that farse should be face and that ace had to be arse and that there was nothing like a white kaffir or white nigger but he wouldn't listen. Men of his specialisation, the country's war heroes, wouldn't listen to anyone. They knew it all and being our MPs and old men, they spent most of their time arguing with the opposition, which only had toddlers and men with no liberation war history (except that of having been sell-outs) in parliament. I could have made him do the calling himself if he knew sufficient English and if he didn't keep on saying tell Baas Kisi this or tell Baas Kisi that.

He had been the white man's tractor driver and he still drove the tractors now though I was unsure of whether it was for Baba Nina, himself or me. That was his other specialisation. Driving tractors. He, like Baba Nina, believed in the prowess of the Englishman's education, which was my own specialisation. I had gone all the way, according to them, though I could never tell them that half the time we had never had any lecturers since they had all gone where the fields were greener and lusher. Or we would be boycotting classes ourselves because of the inadequate government payouts to 'poor' students, or joining into any one of the unsuccessful demonstrations organised by the opposition parties. No, I could never tell them that because they believed in my ability to solve our problems.

So when I had taught them what the father of mass production had told me in those economics textbooks, they had abandoned everything they had ever known before. They had agreed that they'd never thought *mushandirapamwe* in which everyone worked together would succeed. Everyone had to do what they knew best. And that much we did. Baba Nina drove the truck. And Chimoto ploughed the fields. Mama Nina sowed the roundnuts and groundnuts because these were a woman's crops and I sowed the maize. The children, Baba Nina's children, weeded the fields.

We reached the plateau with a final sigh of relief. Chimoto had started to complain that his leg was hurting. I did not see the spring, just as I had failed to see the farm workers in the compound the morning after we had told them we would be taking over the farm and them. We had woken up to find the whole place deserted, as if they had all been some sacred vanishing spring. Instead, I saw a spot where I thought the spring had been, nothing but a ring of stones that could only have signified a fireplace in any ordinary home. 'This is a bad omen,' Chimoto mumbled almost inaudibly.

'What?' Baba Nina asked, his face skewed into a frown. 'I said this is a bad omen,' Chimoto shouted back. I could sense that he was growing agitated. We all kept quiet and he went on talking when he realised no one was going to ask him why. 'If the spring vanishes when you arrive, the mediator will not see you. Don't you know that?'

'Can't you see it's just the drought?' I asked knowing Chimoto would never agree to any such nonsense. He just dismissed me with a flick of his hand.

The door of the lone hut that occupied the plateau stood slightly ajar. Smoke was escaping through every available escape route from the inside of the small mud, pole and grass affair. I saw the door open wider and someone, whose eyes seemed to be red, not from the smoke but from one too many lungfuls of *ganja*, came out. I could tell because the weed had been popular with most students; particularly those of us who thought we had one or two choice words for the government that had failed everyone and the university administration which was nothing but a puppet of that government. It needed guts to stand and call everyone you knew that held not only your future but your life in their hands, a dog and any other such words as would make our mothers shameful of having borne us, if they ever heard that we'd spoken them. The *ganja* gave us all the blindness we needed to face our adversaries head-on, even when they came in armoured cars.

Despite those bloodshot eyes everything about the man suggested that he'd mastered the art of indifference. Maybe that was his specialisation. I could tell he had seen others like us. Hypocrites who came to visit the medium when they thought no one would ever hear about it. But despite his indifference, the man was young and extremely ugly. I could hear Baba Nina smothering a bout of laughter. I nudged him in the ribs and whispered, 'Don't you dare.' The man said 'Hi,' in English, but kept his hands behind his back like a Catholic cleric at confession, as he looked dismissively at our extended hands. We looked at each other and simultaneously withdrew our hands, though not without a little shame.

And then he said, 'I am *sekuru's* assistant.' I couldn't tell whether his remark was accompanied by a grin or a sneer, but I realised that his expression had not lost its indifference. So I didn't know whether he was glad or pissed off about being the mediator's assistant. And since he was looking me in the eye as if with a faint hint of recognition, I grinned at him, almost the grin one would expect to give when caught pants down with another man, behind the church alter.

'What brings you here, *vazukuru*?' he said, abandoning the Englishman's language, as if thinking pained him. I could almost forgive him. After all, his job was not to think but merely translate the unintelligible words of those above as the medium roared them out.

Chimoto looked at Baba Nina. Baba Nina looked at me and I could feel the intensity of his eyes, as if imploring me to find a solution from the Englishman's books I had so gullibly swallowed. But I'd never been to a spirit medium before and nor would I risk annoying the ancestors in their lairs. I looked at the ground. Baba Nina did no better. Besides cleaning cars, the only other thing he knew how to do well was drinking himself stupid and making Mama Nina pregnant. This was why she never got to do very well in her assigned specialisation, she was always either sick or heavy. By now she was carrying their tenth child. So Chimoto had to speak for us.

'We want to see Sekuru.' The assistant looked at Chimoto with indifference. Finally he spoke, the words coming out as if they had been fired from a machine gun. 'Everyone comes here to see *sekuru*. Everyone. Just say why you have come.'

'It's our farm. And it is dying.' Chimoto's voice had lost all its bravado. It was not the voice I heard when he spoke at rallies condemning anyone who opposed the government. This was the other thing I could never tell them. That we had supported the opposition parties and sacrificed our lives when we joined in their planned demonstrations. Even the teargas we had begun to call UBA perfume (which simply meant perfume for the university bachelors associates) and the bullets did not scare us at all. His voice quavered as if he would break down any minute and start to cry.

'Then go and work hard, *vazukuru*. Simply work hard.' For a moment Chimoto did not reply. He turned to look at me, for Baba Nina and I had taken a few steps back after the greeting. Realising that he could not draw anything out of our blank faces, he turned to the assistant but remained quiet.

I knew what he could have said then. That we were working extremely hard. That this year alone, he would have ploughed all the fields, that is if the diesel hadn't run out. That I was progressing very well with the planting of the maize and Mama Nina was doing well despite her condition. Even the children had covered more than what we thought they could. It was only the rains that were letting us down, the ancestors who were refusing to let the heavens open up. He could even have told the assistant what I had taught them all those nights in our study – the study full of the books Baas Kisi had left behind. He could have told him everything, but he chose silence.

We did not talk as we walked back to the car. Somehow I remembered hearing the medium's assistant saying that we couldn't talk to the medium for one or another reason. But it had nothing to do with a spring that had vanished nor did it have anything to do with the medium having gone to a government function. Because after all these years, our war heroes had suddenly remembered that they still needed the ancestors' specialist protection against their enemies (an opposition that wanted to get all of them out of power, not the former white colonists). He stated it all in that indifferent staccato voice of his and hadn't even bothered to reply when I thought I heard Chimoto inquiring when we could come back.

Even then, I was doubtful whether I would traverse this road again, but maybe I would, not to see the medium, but his assistant because I thought that I had once seen him at university. Then he'd seemed an enthusiastic student with a good future in the specialist field of psychology, if there were any jobs for him when he graduated. The money we'd intended to give *sekuru* lay heavy in my pocket, and I ran back to where the spring ought to have been and placed it there. Taking one final look before I descended the mountain, I saw him pick it up, count it and shout 'AHOY', which was the UBA salute, in a tone that had no indifference at all. In fact it contained all the triumph that we felt at Hunger Square after another successful demolition of our halls of residence, complaining of poor living conditions.

I remembered that we – Chimoto, Baba Nina and I – had forgotten to find someone who knew about irrigation. Someone who would wake up each morning with the same gusto as we did to do what they had to do. Our dam was still full and the irrigation equipment was lying idle. Maybe specialisation could work after all, if only we could find someone with the right skills to join us.

Mpofu's Sleep

Brian Jones

It was Mpofu banging at the door, and it was 3.00 a.m. on a wet windy night in December.

'What's wrong,' I shouted from behind the solid wood, burglar-proof door, for this was Zimbabwe at the start of the twenty-first century.

'They've taken the rabbits.'

I unbolted and unlocked the door and looked out through the bars. Mpofu stood there under the security lights, looking even worse than usual. There was blood and dirt on the side of his face, and on his bare feet.

'There were three of them. I ran after them and grabbed one, but I tripped and fell and they got away. I cut my feet.'

Mpofu was in his late forties, but looked twenty years older – he was simply known as Madala by everyone in the neighbourhood. He must have been quite a big, solid man when he was younger, but the wear and tear of life, plus the virus, had taken their toll. He had been sleeping in a hut by the animal pens when we arrived on the plot in Warrington some three years ago and we didn't have the heart to kick him out. His job was 'to guard the animals at night'. This involved sleeping in his hut, as always, but with the door open, so that if anything happened – a snake, a genet, a wild pig or a human visiting the chickens, the rabbits or the vegetables – his wife, MaDube, would rouse him so that he could make lots of noise and frighten the visitors away, or so we hoped. I never imagined that he would go so far as to tackle any of the local poachers.

Mpofu had been born in Sankonjana, close to the Botswana border, a hot dry area some four hours drive through the dust. Like all the males in the area, he had left to try and make his fortune elsewhere, initially as a 'garden boy' in Bulawayo. But he had moved on every few years to various other jobs – in factories and homes in Harare, Masvingo, Mutare, South Africa and Botswana. His education at the local Salvation Army Church school had been very short. He never learnt to read, though he often enjoyed demonstrating to me that he could get by in at least ten languages – Ndebele, Shona, Sotho, Kalanga, Tswana, Zulu, Xhosa, Afrikaans, Tonga and English – not that I understood more than one myself. He'd also never got anywhere near to making his fortune, partly because he'd never listened to his teachers and had drunk much of his earnings. Lately, he had found God and had given up the demon drink for tea, but that didn't stop his serial bigamy, not that he formally married any of his wives, even in the traditional sense. His ex-'wives', including his second wife, MaNcube, who lived locally, often tried to get him to support their children, but he denied that any of them were his, except for his twenty-five year old son Biggie. He had recently started to become restless again – three years in one place was too long for him – and he talked frequently of going to Egoli. 'Biggie could get me work'. He refused to acknowledge his rapidly deteriorating health: it was just 'the dust' or 'no meat' which caused his coughing and his diarrhoea.

He shuffled as he walked along with a bent back, the result of his misfortune in wandering across the unmarked Botswana border in early 1986, on his way home to Sankonjana. The Fifth Brigade happened to be in the area at the time and had taken him to Bhalagwe camp for 'questioning'. Mpofu had no real interest in politics, but he spent the next eleven months being beaten each day, listening to the cries and screams of others. He still bore the marks, physical and mental, of that experience.

Mpofu and I had become close over the few years I had known him. We'd spent many hours drinking our tea together, warming ourselves in the early morning sunshine. He'd tried to teach me a different useful phrase in one of his languages each day – he seemed particularly concerned that I, a white person in Southern Africa, could not speak any Afrikaans – but I'd forget them before the next morning. I tried to teach him a few phrases from my limited knowledge of French; he, of course, picked the phrases up immediately. He became keen for me to bring a French speaker to Warrington so that he could

· ask the time of day, or for directions to the nearest croissant shop.

As the rabbit robbers had just made their getaway, it seemed a good idea to have the police look around those of the neighbours we suspected of acquiring items that did not belong to them. The telephone was working, a fairly rare event in 2007.

'Good morning, is that Kenton police?'

'Uh?'

'Is that Kenton police?'

'Yes sir. How are you this morning?'

'I'm fine, how are you?'

'I'm fine also.'

'I've just had animals stolen. Could you come and help me look for the thieves?'

'How many cattle were taken?'

'It was four rabbits.'

'What?'

'Rabbits. Four of them.'

'Oh. You'd better come in and file a report after eight.'

'But I think I know who took them. Perhaps we could save them.'

'We've got no transport.'

'But I could fetch you.'

After a long delay, the policeman reluctantly agreed that I could pick him up, provided I took him back later. So I left Mpofu to tidy himself up and clean his wounds and drove the ten kilometres to pick up Detective Dube, who was dressed smartly in civilian clothes, but clutched a pistol in his right hand. I noticed a youth of fourteen or so in the police hut, handcuffed by both hands to the legs of the desk – what heinous crime had he committed? Another two men were at the desk with Dube's colleague, writing out an application for a post-mortem, by candlelight as ZESA had failed again.

We returned home to find Mpofu standing at the scene of the crime, looking just a little better.

'Is this the thief?' cried Dube, with a menacing look. Perhaps Mpofu had that affect on those in authority.

After a fruitless inspection around the pens for footprints, and fruitful negotiations as to the sale of a few chickens at a 'good' price to Dube, we, Dube, Mpofu and I, set off in the car to visit the Nyoni brothers, who lived in a crumbling three-roomed house on the next plot. Everyone in the neighbourhood suspected the Nyoni brothers of every theft that had ever taken place, though they'd only ever been arrested for fighting late on Saturday nights at the nearby Collin's Cocktail Bar. We'd visited their house two days before with our other neighbour, Ngwenya, in a fruitless search for his missing garden hose.

There was a light on inside the Nyoni house. We parked the car, and Dube drew his gun.

'Wait here,' he said, 'there's something going on.'

He slid out of the passenger door, gun at the ready, and disappeared into the bush. I waited, nervously; Mpofu had dozed off in the back seat.

Five minutes later Dube was back, breathless. 'He ran into the house, come with me!'

More nervously still, I followed, somewhat unwilling to be involved in a gun battle, even if it would save my four rabbits from certain death. Mpofu, sensibly, remained asleep.

Bursting through the front door, with me well behind, Dube shouted, 'Police. Stay where you are!'

Themba Nyoni stood just inside the front door, fully dressed, his rasta hair perhaps a little dishevelled. His brother, Gift, with a shaven head, hovered by the door to his room, further back. Dube shouted at them in Ndebele, far too fast for me to understand, and the two brothers continued to stand stock-still, looking themselves rather nervous.

'We'll search this room first,' Dube said to me, leading myself and Themba into the first bedroom. Amazingly, two men, seemingly sleeping, lay in two beds in the room. The third ruffled bed was apparently Themba's. There was no evidence of rabbit.

As we left the room, Dube yelled, 'After him!' and rushed after Gift who was disappearing fast through the back door.

I decided to stay where I was, hopefully a bit safer away from Dube and his gun, though conversation with Themba was a bit stilted.

Dube returned after a few minutes, limping a little. 'The skellum got away, let's search his room.'

There was just one bed in the tiny room, a blanket thrown across it, though there was an enormous freezer in the narrow, adjacent corridor. I opened the freezer lid with trepidation, expecting to see my poor rabbits already dispatched and ready for braaiing. But the freezer was empty.

Having glanced around the bedroom, I announced, 'Nothing here either,' and made to leave.

'Wait,' said Dube. 'There's a funny smell in here.'

I too noticed the unpleasant aroma of death, just as Dube pulled back the blanket to reveal the carcass of a butchered goat. The flesh had been removed from the body, leaving only a skeleton with its feet and the head intact. But no rabbits.

Dube shouted at Themba for several minutes, and Themba explained that Gift was the culprit. He had hidden the goat in the bed, and then run away when it was clear we'd find it. Themba professed to know nothing about rabbits.

It didn't make a difference. Dube decided to arrest Themba anyway, presumably on the grounds that it was an offence to be related to a poacher. So, taking the evidence with us (perhaps for goat stew the next day), we headed back to the police post.

Themba was handcuffed to the desk in the hut – the youth must have been taken away somewhere – but Dube decided it would be best if Mpofu and I returned in a day or two to file a report, as there was no paper left. 'Maybe some will come tomorrow.' There was a slight problem, as he was required to write down an incident number for me, which he resolved writing on one of his Z$1,000 dollar notes. 'It's not worth anything anyway,' he said with a shrug.

I drove back home to allow Mpofu to continue his sleep alone in his hut, his wife having already risen to go vegetable picking on Esat's nearby farm. Having found bread at Lucky Seven Supermarket the day before, I settled for tea and toast, a rare treat. Then I headed off to work.

I returned at 5.00 p.m. to find lots of people huddled at the gate. MaDube came screaming towards me shouting 'Do something! Do something!' and I spotted Mpofu lying in my wheelbarrow in the middle of the huddle. He wasn't moving and was very pale. He didn't look at all well to me; in fact, he looked dead. Apparently, around lunchtime, he'd been visiting MaNcube, his ex-wife who lived a kilometre or so away, and had collapsed. Presumably she didn't want her new husband to find Mpofu there and had arranged for her two teenage sons (who were probably also Mpofu's) to collect him in the wheelbarrow. Themba Nyoni was there too, urging me to take Mpofu to the 'Accident and Emergency' – he'd been released from custody after his lunch (of goat stew?) because of 'lack of evidence'.

I didn't think there was any emergency, if there had been, it was over, but I could see no alternative to using the last of my scarce petrol to take Mpofu to hospital. Of course, his family had to come too, so we fitted the stiffening Mpofu between his two wives on the back seat, while his two sons squeezed onto the front seat. Luckily, we were waved through the ubiquitous police roadblocks and arrived at 'Accident and Emergency' without mishap. The sons rushed off and returned, amazingly quickly, with a functioning wheelchair and we pushed Mpofu towards the formidable looking nurse behind the desk.

She glanced quickly at the comatose figure. 'You'll have to wait over there for a doctor, there isn't one here at the moment.'

We sat, the five of us, on a hard bench, Mpofu upright in his wheelchair. It was half an hour before I braved the nurse again.

'I'm sure he's dead, can't you talk to the family and explain, please? They're in a terrible state.'

'Who do you think you are? A doctor? Only a doctor can tell if a person is dead. Go back and wait.'

So we sat there, me knowing that it made no difference, them too intimidated to complain, watching patients in various states of accident and emergency come in and be told to 'Wait' by the nurse. It was now approaching 8 p.m., the room was filling fast, and I was hungry and tired, so I approached the nurse again.

'Please, can't you get a doctor to look at Mpofu, his family are really worried.'

'What's the point of a doctor looking at him? He's dead!'

'Then, please, will you tell them.'

'It's not my job.'

After pleading with her for what seemed like an age, she came from behind the desk and walked purposefully towards MaDube, MaNcube and the two sons, who looked up expectantly.

'He's dead.' She turned and went back to her desk.

African Laughter

Rory Kilalea

- One Thatched hut
- Three Lions
- Two Black actors
- One Rhino
- One Black Arb (Arbitrary extra)
- Loin skins for black actors
- One white actor
- Oil for black actors
- Spears and feather head-dresses for black actors
- Scrawny chickens
- One *mombi*
- Friends in the National Parks open to bribes for film permissions.

AFRICAN FILMMAKERS MUST HAVE the above when an international crew wants to set up their film. The foreign producers may be liberal. They may even wear leather sandals. They may be lumpy, drink a great deal of gin and drive a Porsche with a Jewish registration. But the true story is – they will all have a satisfied look that they are really changing the planet. And they will insist on all of the above.

That's the way it is.

My last job – arrange a drama documentary of True Stories – real life escapes in the African wild for a UK television network.

So it was the normal type of thing.

- Bribes for Locations at the Mana Pools.

Get the actors ...

• Wiener – fluent in three languages and women.

• Walter – a Paramount Chief who fled the rigours of rural life to manage the Zimbabwean Football team because of the kickbacks.

• His cousin (playing the Black Arb).

• And there was me.

Now that is not how it normally happens. I never appear in front of the screen, as I could be recognised. Then the game would be up forever. But this time they wanted a ragged-looking white Zimbo, between forty and death who could act. A local actor would not require a first-class ticket from London, or stay at the Sheraton.

As there are only about five ragged white males left in our country – and I knew them all from Reps, the Keg and the Bowling Club – it should have been easy. But none could act. Sure they can bluster, be aggro about government and all of that away from the marauding Green Bombers – but they cannot *really* act.

The producers did not know it was me. I called myself Didymus.

I changed my name from Thomas to get extra money for the acting as well as being facilitator. I prepared my costume: khaki pants and shirt, an Akubra hat, and a pair of brown Raybans. I spent a lot of time with my ragged friends at Reps bar and stopped shaving for a week. I looked suitably bushy-fied.

• Get the crew ...

Our location manager was Colin – the only man for this job. He knew how to manage toilets near the Zambezi and put up the tents for the precious overseas crew. He had a strong relationship with his digging crew (for the long drops), and was efficient in arranging chemicals that were user friendly and, more importantly still, in ordering the mobile honey wagon (toilets) to take secret trips into the Game Park to dispose of the waste. He also knew how to use a gun. Colin was ideal, even though he was white – but the overseas crew knew that above all political considerations, *teas and toilets* were essential in a black country.

It was all going to be one hundred per cent.

Colin would meet the crew at the airport, and then convoy the trucks up to the Zambezi Valley. An amazing man for 54, Colin is easily recognised. A long-distance runner who smokes 60 Madison cigarettes a day. Colin also wears his denim shorts so tight they're like a condom. The UK crew would know who he was. He loves his black Zimbabwean crew like a family, but he does not like black people in general.

That's the way it is in Zimbabwe.

• Get the animals …

I hired wild animals from a man who has an annoying habit of taking a deposit and then disappearing. I would travel with him to ensure the animals would make it there. Also, I had to tell him that I was not using my real name, I was Didymus.

'I'll call you anything you want, *jy Moer!* Just make sure you get the bleddy money in my bank!'

Negotiating with him was tricky. He argued for hours, insisted the money was in forex and then presented another bill on the shooting day – blackmailing the foreigners to pay before his animals performed. There were also rumours that he was paying kickbacks to producers to get the jobs. He was making a fortune. He was South African.

The river was sluggishly beautiful, haunting sounds of the fish eagles vaunting overhead, hippos grunting their territory, waterbucks wandering by … all wondering what the hell Condom Colin was doing, digging shit holes, setting up tents and cameras.

The dust alerted us to the Royal Arrival.

'Hello,' I smiled.

The director was tall and had a haunted look from the overnight flight in Air Zimbabwe business class.

The producer turned out to be a woman.

It was the producer from the Bahamas with very large legs. A producer I had worked with some years before. A producer who had taken advantage of me with those Bahamian Baobabs. A producer who knew me.

'Hello, Thom …' She started, before I swept her off her feet into an all-embracing mouth-smothering kiss.

'I am Didymus.' I slobbered between gulps of air.

The Bahamian Baobabs relaxed a little.

'You know each other?' asked the director.

'Met once,' she said. 'This is Didymus.' And kept my hands on her legs.

'Fab! Brill! You look delightfully *rough* … *love* the bags under the eyes …'

'Lost someone in the family,' I said.

'Cannot thank you enough for coming out of mourning …' the director retorted.

I smiled.

'Where's Thomas? I arranged everything with him. He must be here!'

Silence. This was going to be difficult. *I* was Thomas – but I was also Didymus.

Had not thought of that.

'Want to thank him. It all looks *so* professional,' gushed the director.

Pause.

'He's dead,' said the producer.

'Is it catching?'

'Don't worry.' She smiled at me. 'He's buried.'

Things were going well.

'This is Wiener … the black actor for the hut scene,' I said.

'Sounds like a sausage,' giggled the director.

'Very funny,' said Wiener. (He has since changed his name, now that he lives in London, as a lot of really stupid English people said the same thing.)

'Wieners are large here,' said Walter. The director winked.

'This is Walter, the black rhino hero.' I said, very quickly.

'Actually, it is a white rhino,' said the untrustworthy animal handler.

'I knew that,' I said haughtily. 'I meant that Walter is black.'

'I can see that,' giggled the director.

'Hullo, Baas,' said Walter in a *very* rural accent.

'Walter!' I hissed. '*Stop* it.'

Walter ignored me, smiled at the director. 'Hello *baasie baasie!*'

The director looked nonplussed.

'PLEASE, you must not call me Boss …'

Walter scratched his head, picked his nose and then said, 'But if you are not the Baas … I am not a rhino!'

'Oh no … ' deprecated the Director, his hands in a dither.

'And this …' I said, glaring at Walter.

'Is the black Arb …' smiled Wiener at the cousin three times removed.

'I am Hapless,' he said.

'Oh no … you are one of the heroes …' smiled the director.

'But my name is Hapless …' frowned the cousin.

'Perfect,' stuttered the director. 'See you at dinner.' And he stumbled off to his tent to sleep.

'We have only THREE DAYS!' I yelled at the producer. 'What about the sunset shots?'

'We like big women,' said Wiener, watching her examining the Ariflex 3, canoes and things that producers do.

As the day began to wane, and the sky turned pink and orange, as the hippos vied with the frogs for mating calls, the producer simply did all of the director's work. She carried tons of equipment, filmed the postcard shots, did close-ups of crocs watching us watching them, woman-handled the canoe into a backlit beauty shot, and then loaded all of the gear onto her back.

'Must have a G and T,' she said, massaging her legs.

'Of course,' I said and poured her a triple. A hippo called in the distance.

'I love the raw sounds of Africa,' she said.

She addressed us around the trestle table under an Acacia, as if we were in an office in London. The white tablecloth, the silverware, the crystal that I had organised was ignored. Producers do that and it really hurts.

'First of all we will start with Didymus and the Rhino. Then we will do Wiener and the lions …'

The director emerged, wearing open sandals and duty-free cologne. Strong smells like that can attract insects and things.

By the time he sat down, his feet had been explored by a few baboon spiders, centipedes and a rather attractive lizard. He was in a state of high tension when the tomato soup (garnished with biltong) arrived.

By the time the roast warthog was carved and settled on his plate, his face was a mass of pink and red blotches from the bombing mozzies.

'You *have* taken your anti-malarials?' snapped the producer.

'Must get my pills,' he said, swatting at everything in sight.

The director jumped up and ran off to his tent without a flashlight or a guide.

'Hope he finds his way,' Colin smiled.

We were on pudding when we heard a couple of low coughs from the bush nearby. But heck … this was the Mana Pools … of course we would hear wild animals. Part of the charm.

'Better check on the director,' said the producer, pouring herself another G and T.

I sighed, and with Colin the Condom (and his three-foot Mag Light), checked on the Creative Talent.

The director had the gas lamp burning brightly inside his tent. We could see his shape huddled in a tight silhouette. Trembling a little. Like a low budget horror movie. The tent was firmly zipped shut.

'You all right?' I asked.

'Yes ...' An octave higher than normal.

'Pudding is waiting,' I said.

'Don't want to!' He said.

'Very good mango ice-cream!' I tempted.

'Won't! Don't want to!' Petulant.

'Come out now,' ordered Condom Colin.

'Won't!' he said.

'Then fuck yourself,' muttered Condom Colin.

'G'night,' I said, as we walked over the lion tracks outside his tent.

'They circled the whole tent,' said Condom Colin.

'Love the Mana,' I said.

'How is he?' asked the producer.

'Resting.' We finished dinner in normal African style, sitting around the smouldering coals, watching the stars, listening to the predators and the occasional lapping of the crocs in the river, washed down with more G and T's.

That was the end of night one.

Dawn was called and we scurried to a quick exploding egg sandwich and a cup of coffee as the day's work began.

It was my big day. It was easy really. All I had to do was act the part of a film producer who wanted the best photograph of a rhino. With his trusty black guide, Walter, and a Hapless bearer (the Arb), we were to tramp through the bush. At a certain cue, given by the crooked animal handler, I was supposed to flash my camera and the rhino would charge. Walter would heroically save my life by hanging onto the underbelly of the grey creature, and steering it into the trees. Hapless Black would cheer and do African dancing.

'Is this a true story?' I asked.

'Yes,' said the director. '*Brill!* Really *Brill!*'

'Sounds like horse shit to me,' said Condom Colin.

'Nobody mentioned stunt rhinos' said the animal handler. 'Need more money for that.'

'Who is this arse-hole?' said Walter.

'That's the way it is …' I shrugged.

While the producer negotiated with the animal handler, the director chose the best place to film. It was spectacular. Right in the middle of the acacia forest (not that rhinos browse there), it was flat enough for the rhino to charge.

'*Simply begs* to be filmed,' said the director.

A smiling animal handler returned with the rhino, clucking it into a financially advantageous position.

'Take One …'

I chatted amiably to Walter and Hapless Black as we sauntered through the forest.

'CUT!'

'What's wrong?' I said.

'Didymus … you're a WHITE producer …' Shouted the director.

'Yes?'

'Be realistic! You DON'T TALK to BLACKS!"

'What's he on about?' said Walter.

'Blacks DON'T TALK to WHITES!'

The director spoke loudly with emphasis.

'I want some of what he's smoking,' said Wiener.

By Take Five, I had it right. I looked east, and west, always avoiding the eyes of Hapless Black, trying not to laugh at Walter, oiled in a loin skin, leopard-crawling to show that he was a good tracker.

'PRINT!' Shouted the director.

'Nearly done. One tracking shot of the whole sequence.' The producer winked at me. 'And then some minor close ups.'

We were ahead of schedule.

The second shot was trickier. From a different angle, with our arms and legs in the same positions (for continuity) we approached a copse of trees. This was where I see the rhino and flash the camera at it.

My cues …

• Signal One – notice the rhino – then flash the camera.

• Signal Two – run from rhino.

• Signal Three – Hapless Black would run away.

• Signal Four – Walter would, as any loyal black, leap under the charging animal and save me.

'Turn Over!'

Hapless and I went forward. I walked like the Pink Panther.

Walter ignored my method acting.

• Signal One.

I looked up, and saw the Rhino. Pause. Use the moment. FLASH! Great! … It was working.

• Signal Two.

The rhino began charging me. Hapless looked suitably terrified. For good reason. My foot was stuck in an ant-bear hole!

'Stick to the day job,' Walter suggested.

The beast was nearer! Fuck! Hapless started sweating a lot. 'Pull that foot out Thomas!' he yelled.

• Signal Three

Screams from the director. Hapless tried to run. But he could not. The pounding tons of grey animal with an aphrodisiac on its mullet remain with him today.

'Ack!' I bellowed and threw the camera at the rhino.

A rhino being beaned by a camera is not a good move. It makes animals cross.

• Signal Four

'Kill the damn thing!' I screamed at the animal handler. He smirked.

Walter stood his ground, just like paramount chiefs are supposed to. Hapless ran to the right, yelling and waving his spear.

'So loyal, these blacks!' screamed the director.

The rhino swerved past me and went for Hapless. He danced around, springing and looking very impressive. Then Walter, in a fluid movement, jumped under the rhino … one arm wrapped around a horn, and disappeared into the acacias. Hapless Black was still bouncing around in panic.

'*Brilliant!*' gushed the director. Within minutes, our close-ups were done, and the rhino was in his boma munching away.

Hapless Black has never liked British Whites ever since that day.

'Thanks, *shamwari!*' I said to Walter.

'Anytime.'

The Baobab licked her lips.

The director was so impressed with Walter; that he put him into the next sequence. This was the 'true' story of two black men trapped by hungry lions in their village.

We got the set ready. A novel experience for Africans. Viewers who have never set foot on the continent have this 'African Queen' idea.

Round thatched huts, lots of cow dung, pieces of sticks which are supposed to be for storing maize or something, and chickens. You must also have a cow, or as we know it, a *mombi*. (The USA likes naked Masai drinking milk and blood.)

The hut has to be terracotta with aged thatch, and unless you are forceful, normally has ridiculous primitive paintings on the walls. The huts also have to be under a tree. Truth does not come into this equation – true huts are not under trees (as snakes drop onto the roof), storage bins are solid, designed to deter rats, and money is used for seed, not primitive paintings.

But there you are.

Our job was to make the set look like a true example of how the Noble Savage can exist in Nature. Meanwhile, crooked animal handler groomed the three lions.

Wiener and Walter were in fine fettle. They had sneaked into the catering store and been drinking beers. It's very hot in the Zambezi Valley.

As with the other 'true stories', Wiener and Walter had to be dressed in loin skins, oiled up – that entire sort of '300' camera friendly thing. 'Now ... darlings ... said the director, 'what you do ... is come out of the hut ... stretch as if you've had a good night's sleep, and then suddenly see these two simply *ferocious* lions ...'

'S'easy,' slurred Wiener.

'Yes, Baasie,' said Walter, hiding his beer bottle under his loins.

'Then ... you clamber up to the top of the hut... and watch in *horror!* While the lions stalk you ...'

'Umm...wouldn't the lions go for the cow?' I said.

'I KNOW what I'm doing ... I've been stalked by lions ...' Glare from the director. 'Like last night! MAN EATERS!'

'Man s'eaters ...' drawled Wiener.

'YES! *Yes Wiener!*' The director was ecstatic. (Walter thinks the director has the hots for Wiener.)

'The lions go round and round ... for days ... we will do this in post production of course ...' continued the director. 'Then you leap to the tree and escape!'

'When they're not looking ...' added Wiener.

'Like baboons...' barked Walter archly.

'YES ...' Another seductive smile to Wiener.

'Brilliant!' echoed Walter.

'This story is horseshit!' spat Condom Colin.

'Lions are ready,' yelled the Handler.

I sat beside the monitor while the director framed the shots and occasionally scratched his mozzie bites (he had socks under his sandals, like a missionary).

'Shall we rehearse?' said the director.

'No ... The lions get tired in the heat of the day,' said the crooked animal handler. 'Can't act when they are tired.'

'Animals don't *act*!' muttered Colin.

'We must do a take!' insisted the animal handler. He wanted to go home and check his bank account.

'Two cameras ready?' ordered the Producer.

And this is the way it was.

Walter and Wiener were superb. Either booze or acting skills. They were unsteady on their feet as they emerged from the gloom of the hut into the stark sunlight. They stretched, farted and yawned. Then the director turned to me and said, 'Is that normal?'

'What?' I said.

'Look!'

Wiener and Walter had decided not to wear underpants.

'Lucky them ...' said the producer.

I nodded as if it was the most natural thing in the world.

At a sharp command from the handler, the lions bounded forward. Wiener and Walter suddenly started, wakened from their malted stupor. They clambered, buttocks and appendages heaving, until they were at the top of the hut. They began wailing and yelling, eyes rolling, arms flailing, and looking really terrified.

'Aren't they a little too Sambo?' said the Producer.

'What?'

'Walter and Wiener are really acting their loins off!'

Then I noticed that the crooked animal handler was aiming a rifle at them.

'What the hell is he doing?'

'Ask someone who cares,' said the director. 'I only wanted three lions ... look ... I've got TEN!'

A pride of lions had come up the bank to check out our three trained felines. They made a frantic charge at each other. The animal handler fired a shot in the air.

The lions attacked the cow. The other lions clawed at the hut, roaring. Wiener prayed to his ancestors for redemption. Walter sprayed beer at their eyes.

Another shot in the air!

The crooked animal handler advanced like Rambo. The lions looked baffled. Some cocked their heads up from the dead cow, the females circled, he stood stoically still.

'Camera One ... get the Animal Handler saving the poor uncivilised blacks!' shouted the director.

Camera Two swung around to get a shot of Walter and Wiener skittering up the nearest tree.

'Close ups!' yelled the director in orgasm, amidst the yawing sound of hungry lions at a bloody *mombi* and Rambo with his rifle.

It all ended with the crooked animal handler firing another shot at the paws of the lions, and they fled.

Including his trained predators.

'Close ups of the blacks!' yelled the director. Both cameras trained on Wiener and Walter in the tree.

'More emotion!' screamed the director.

'Yes, baasie,' they said, and did imitations of frightened baboons.

'STOP!' I yelled.

'Pardon?' said the producer and the director together.

'You are paternalistic, son-of-a-bitch-users!' I yelled.

'Excuse me?' said the director quietly.

'Risking the lives of our people ... our Zimbabweans ... for a stupid neo-paternalistic piece of fiction ...' I spluttered.

'I am the director,' came the fluid vowels ... 'I can do what I want!' (He must have been related to our president.)

'Bloody royal dick head,' I said in a lofty fashion. 'You don't know nothing!'

'Gays gangsters!' slurred Wiener.

'And...' said Condom Colin ... 'you Brits are a waste of rations!'

'It's not a true story at all!' said Walter.

'Frankly... I don't care what you think,' said the director. 'I've got what I want.'

'Cunt head!' I yelled after him, hoping he would get scorpions in his socks.

'Wiener – come to my tent to discuss some notes on acting would you?' smiled the director.

'I'm getting my blacks home!' said Colin.

'Top chaps, really' said Walter as he adjusted his loincloth.

'I've lost three lions,' frowned the crooked animal handler.

The producer went off to negotiate.

'Let's have a beer, *shamwari!*' offered Walter.

'Will Wiener be all right?' I asked.

'Of course *shamwari* – if the director tries anything illegal, Wiener will blackmail him – we'll have more money!'

We sauntered over to the booze tent.

That last night at the camp, when I had taken my biltong soup (with a fricassee of tomato) the producer unzipped my tent in a practiced fashion and told me ...

• I was a total ass.

• I would not get my acting fees.

• I would not get my production fees as the loss of lions had blown the budget.

• Unless ...

That was when I decided that I would continue my career in films in Africa. I really liked Bahamian Baobabs. I also like hippos, producers and directors. I love Africa.

So I did get my fees. With a little extra from Wiener.

I have another film next week. With the same crew. And the untrustworthy animal handler. But this time he will pay me 15% of the gross.

That's the way it is.

A Dirty Game

Daniel Mandishona

IN JANUARY 2003, WHEN I WAS THIRTEEN YEARS OLD, my eldest sister Bernadette sent us an e-mail saying she was planning to marry a Kenyan doctor she had met whilst studying medicine in England. She said the special wedding invite was on its way and the event itself would take place on Boxing Day in an old stone church in a town called Cambridge, which was near London.

My other sister Primrose and myself had never been to England and were very excited by the news of this proposed event. All I knew about Cambridge was that its university was the source of grief for many teenagers because that was where the O-Level exam papers were set. My father, elated by the news that he was finally to have a son-in-law, started making hurried arrangements for the trip even though there was still almost a year to go before the big event.

In 2003 my sister Prim was sixteen years old and in the fourth form at a very expensive Catholic school. Prim was not terribly bright and could never grasp the simplest scientific concepts. Quadratic equations completely baffled her, matrices and geometric transformations made her develop goose bumps and for a long time she couldn't tell the difference between cirrostratus, cirrocumulus and stratocumulus. She also thought mensuration and menstruation were one and the same thing. The only subject she was good at was Fashion and Fabrics, mainly because she spent a fortune on glossy magazines and watched a lot of daytime soap operas.

Even when we watched a film on television Prim was more interested in what the characters were wearing than in the dramatic nuances of the story. She hardly read her books, but preferred to spend her time text-messaging friends on the latest celebrity gossip. She had a pointless but all-consuming interest in the day-to-day adventures of pop and film stars – who was sleeping with who, who had checked into rehab, who had the weirdest sexual fetish and so on and so forth.

Her end-of-term reports – despite diplomatic phrases like 'tries very hard' and 'needs to unlock her true potential' – pointed to a hopeless student firmly on the path to academic oblivion. But this did not deter her; she harboured vague ambitions of being someone very important in the government when she finished school, just like our father. We all knew she wasn't going to do well in her O-levels and had mentally prepared ourselves for the worst. My mother said even if it meant she had to re-write it wouldn't exactly be the end of the world.

'I know many people whose children have failed exams,' she would say. 'Exams don't mean much these days. Some of the world's most successful people were not very good at school. Everybody knows that America, the world's most powerful nation, has had a failed actor as one of its presidents. Prim has her dreams, and that's good enough for me.'

In a way my mother was right. Everyone who is successful must have dreamed of something.

Bernadette has always been the clever one in our family. In her younger years we used to call her 'Brain Box', a nickname she loathed with a passion. She won prizes from Grade One to Grade Seven and sailed through secondary school. She achieved a record breaking five 'A's at A-Level, which was how she had won a Rhodes scholarship to study medicine in England. She had even overcome that other notorious pitfall of teenage-hood, the driving test, at her very first attempt.

I remember how at the time she won the scholarship my father greeted the news of her achievement with mixed feelings. On the one hand he was happy for his daughter's good fortune but on the other hand, as a senior government official, he resented the fact that her benefactor was none other than that infamous British colonialist, Cecil John Rhodes, an individual whose exploitative and manipulative skills my father put in the same mould as those of history's worst blackguards – Hitler, Napoleon, Stalin, Bismarck. My father didn't like the British, always telling us that they were thieves and plunderers who had stolen the black man's wealth under the guise of religious philanthropy.

'It was the arrival of the Bible that put the black man in chains,' he would moan.

Both Prim and I had gone on holidays with our parents before, but only to regional destinations like Mauritius, Johannesburg, Cape Town and Durban. Because of his important job in the government my father had been to every place on earth that could be reached by passenger plane – Singapore, Guatemala, Malaysia, Egypt, China, Dubai, Bhutan. He once went to Egypt and told us that a blind beggar showed him the exact spot where Moses had parted the Red Sea to escape Pharaoh's wrath. He had even been to Outer Mongolia, a place I only knew as a sprawling mass of hilly outcrops on a relief map of Asia at the school library. But his favourite place was Beijing. He always said the people there were very friendly and the food those Chinese ate was simply amazing. They eat everything, he said, including monkeys, tortoises, sharks, dogs, lizards, cockroaches, cats and snakes. Once, on an official trip to the People's Republic and much the worse for alcohol, he had been daring enough to try racoon meat.

'It tastes like chicken,' he told us on his return.

During the second term school holiday we accompanied my father to the British High Commission to make the visa applications. There were many people outside the building and the queue went twice around the block. In 2003 people in my country had to queue for everything because everything was in short supply. Sugar, milk, salt, cooking oil, fuel and sometimes, even water. Some people we talked to told us they had been in the queue from four o'clock in the morning, waiting to have their papers processed. They had even brought food to eat and novels to read whilst idling away time in the long queue. Our father took one look at the meandering line of bodies, looked at his watch, told us to wait for him and then disappeared inside the building. We were only in the queue for about ten minutes before he came back and asked us to follow him. We immediately knew he had arranged something. My father was a senior government official and he knew many influential people. He always 'arranged' things.

We went into a small office where a balding African gentleman with uneven yellow teeth asked us to fill in some forms while he exchanged idle chat with my father. He asked my father whether he could use his political connections to arrange a large commercial farm for him, preferably one with a large dam or stream running through it.

'With these recurrent droughts irrigation is best,' said the bald man.

My father said it was now difficult to get a farm because of the bad publicity in the press about all the people being given farms and not doing anything with them, but he would see what could be done. The bald man, eager to please his would-be benefactor, said the people who were getting land and not utilising it were unwittingly helping the cause of those committed to derailing the government's agrarian reform programme.

'These people are two-faced. They are wolves wearing sheep's clothes,' said the bald man.

'Yes, they are reactionaries working in cahoots with imperialist forces to reverse the gains of our hard-won Independence,' agreed my father.

But my father did not need a visa to go to England. He had a special government passport that allowed him to visit any country in the world any time he wanted to do so. The bald man asked us to sign our visa application forms. I did not yet have a proper signature so I just made up one on the spot – a scrawny and indeterminate mark that Prim took one look at and shook her head in disbelief. When we left, the queue outside the building was twice its original length. Most of the people in it looked weary and dejected, like a demoralised army on the verge of a catastrophic defeat. I was happy I had a father who knew people and could arrange things.

That evening when we got home our mother showed us some pictures of Benny and her Kenyan boyfriend that had come by e-mail. The pictures had been taken when Benny and the Kenyan man had gone on a walking holiday near some Welsh town with an unpronounceable name. I asked Prim why anybody in England would want to go and walk on their holiday when there were all those cars available but she was in a foul mood and just shook her head and clicked her tongue.

'Just go and do your homework,' she said.

The Kenyan doctor was a handsome fellow, quite unlike his thin and dark countrymen I had seen chasing steeples or running the marathon at the Olympics in Australia. He had an expansive grin on his face, like a man who had just won the Lotto jackpot. But I felt both relieved and jealous that he was everything I had not imagined him to be.

The months slowly went by and in late October my own excitement, which by then far surpassed everybody else's, reached fever pitch. I badly wanted to go to London to see Piccadilly Circus and Big Ben and all the other things I had seen on television. I dreamt of sunset cruises on the Thames and of having my photograph taken standing next to the famous wax figures at Madame Tussaud's. I dreamt of Buckingham Palace and the Tower of London, where our history teacher Mr Gandu told us many members of the nobility had been beheaded for treason and adultery.

'The English used to be ordinary savages,' he explained. 'The French were worse. Did you know they are the ones who invented the guillotine?'

I already knew that, but I didn't want to say so because Mr Gandu would have accused me of showing off. Mr Gandu did not take kindly to his students knowing things he thought they didn't know. But then as the days dragged by I started to worry about unthinkable possibilities, about things that could go wrong when we least expected them to – what our English teacher Mr Brennan called 'Sod's Law'. It was quite possible my father could have an unwelcome attack of his perennial gout problem a day before our scheduled departure. During these attacks the big toe on his right foot would become tender and pink, like an overcooked beetroot, grounding him for several days and forcing him to go on an herbivorous diet. Sometimes the pain would become so bad he could barely walk.

'It's like walking barefoot on a field of broken glass,' was how he often described the excruciating pain.

Mother would give him an unsympathetic look, put her hands on her hips and just shake her head. At supper she would tell me to eat my greens.

'Men and meat and beer… Now you can see where it all ends.'

But we all knew she didn't really mean whatever she said. It was just her way of telling him to watch his eating habits. But he never listened. As soon as he was back on his feet it was back to Zambezi lager, T-bones, fried liver and braised oxtail.

There were other subtle variants of 'Sod's Law' that could yet scupper the big event. What if on the day of our departure the plane was inexplicably cancelled or delayed and we had to postpone our trip? What if there was a nationwide fuel shortage and we couldn't even go to the airport? What if mother suffered one of her momentary amnesia bouts and forgot all our passports and tickets at home? What if the Kenyan doctor developed cold feet and decided that our Benny, incredibly beautiful and intelligent as she was, was not the one for him? What if some Kenyan woman he was secretly married to back home in Nairobi turned up on the day of the wedding and actually stood up during the part when the priest challenges those with objections to the marriage to stand up or forever hold their peace, and didn't hold hers? It had happened before, at the wedding of one of my father's cousins. The man's 'small house' turned up unannounced at the reception and caused untold pandemonium. All these things were quite possible, in my view. We did not know the history of the man Benny wanted to marry and all we could do was place our faith in her judgment and hope for the best. After all, as our father always reminded us, Benny was a sensible girl.

One day at school I told my best friend Robert Nhamo that my sister Benny was having a wedding in a big stone church in England and that all of us were flying there at the beginning of the summer holiday for the occasion. I asked him whether there was anything special he wanted me to bring back and he said his brother Kennedy who lived in England had told him everything there was so expensive maybe the only thing I could afford to bring back for him were chocolates and wine gums from the airport duty-free shops. I said if that were the case I would be happy to just go and see Piccadilly Circus and Big Ben and maybe take pictures on my father's new digital camera to show him. He said I shouldn't get excited for nothing because Piccadilly Circus was not a real circus – there were no lions or trapeze artists or dodgem cars – and Big Ben was just a big clock on a tower at the Houses of Parliament. I could see he was jealous, but he was my friend and I did not mind him feeling the way he did. I could understand his envy.

A week before the wedding my father came home from work early one evening and dropped a bombshell. He said he had gone to the British High Commission to check on our visas and been told by his bald friend with the yellow teeth that there had been a slight problem with our applications. He said all of us would not be going to the wedding in England. He said even his special government passport that allowed him to visit any country in the world at any time he wanted was no good. My mother furrowed her brow in disbelief.

'Surely the British can't do that?'

'It's their country and they can do anything they want.'

'But why?'

My father said an organisation called the European Union had put our country on an international list of bad guys and all the people connected in some way to the government were banned from travelling to Europe.

'But we want to go to Britain, not Europe.' Mother interjected in the shrill but determined voice she used when having pointless arguments with my father.

'Britain is in Europe.'

The ban, father added, included spouses and dependants. My mother, though clearly just as disappointed as all of us, thought she had a simple solution.

'Why don't they have the wedding in America? It would be nice to go to New York or Miami.'

My mother had been to a conference in Miami at the invitation of some non-governmental organisation and she often told us of that city's buildings that were painted in every colour of the rainbow. On her way back from that trip she forgot her camera with all the pictures she had taken in the closet of her hotel room.

'We cannot even go to America,' said father. 'There is another list of banned people there and we are also on it.'

'All of us?'

Father nodded his head.

My mother, undeterred, pressed on.

'If we can't go there, why don't they come here? There are many places here where they can have a decent wedding reception. There is the Sheraton, the Holiday Inn, the Botanical Gardens and even the large hall at my church can be hired for a small fee.'

My father shook his head.

'Benny cannot come here.'

'Why not? This is the country of her birth. Surely, the European Union or whatever it's called can't stop her coming here?'

'I know. But if she comes here she won't be able to go back to England. Her papers there are not in order.'

'In England?'

'Yes.'

'But she has a valid passport ...'

'You need other papers to stay in England – a visa and work permit. It's fine if you don't have those things if you're already there. But once you leave the country you can't go back.'

'But she went there on a Rhodes scholarship ...'

'It doesn't matter. She finished university two years ago. She is now working, and she does not have a work permit.'

'So?'

'That makes her an illegal immigrant. If they catch her, they will deport her.'

My mother clicked her tongue in disgust. She looked perplexed, like a contestant on a quiz show who keeps getting the answers wrong. But she knew all there was to know about deportations, two of her maternal cousins having been expelled from America for being 'illegal aliens'. One of them, aunt Gertrude, had spent twelve years working as a housemaid for a man whose job was to find and prosecute illegal immigrants.

Mother slowly walked to the kitchen where she was preparing a tuna and avocado salad for herself. She always ate tuna and avocado salads during the hot weather because she claimed it was good for her skin. My mother constantly worried about her skin losing its lustre and her body losing its shape. So she always watched what she ate, and told us what to eat. But the news about the visas had clearly unsettled her. She kept blowing her cheeks and shaking her head. She kept complaining about the many things she did not understand that happened in the world. Why was our country on a list of bad guys and yet we had never done any harm to anybody?

My father pointed out that her observation was not quite true. He told her that we had taken the land back from the white people in the country and their kinsmen in the European Union were punishing us for it. It's not their land, my mother protested. The white people found us here.

'That may be so,' said my father, 'but politics is a dirty game.'

Later that evening I asked Prim whether she thought we could get visas for Benny's wedding if the government gave back some of the land it had taken. I explained to her how it could be done. A formula could be worked out whereby, say, each farm returned to a white farmer would result in one visa being given to a prospective traveller. So in the case of the four of us who wanted to go to Benny's wedding, the government would give back four farms to the white people. That way, everybody would be happy. It would be what our English teacher Mr Brennan called a win-win situation.

'Don't be silly. The government is not going to give back the land so you and I can get visas to go to Benny's wedding in England. The government people in England don't even know who Benny is.'

'But our father is a senior government official. Everybody knows him.'

'So?'

Prim always supported the government, through thick and thin – through flood or hail. Maybe it was because she harboured vague ambitions to work for the government when she left school.

'You honestly think anybody else apart from us cares about Benny's wedding?'

'Benny is my sister. I care for her, just like I care for you.'

She clicked her tongue and just glared at me.

'You know something?'

'What?'

'You are a very stupid boy.'

We never went to England.

We stayed at home and waited for news of the wedding. Whenever my mother said how unfair the whole visa thing was my father would just shake his head and tell her that politics was a dirty game. Even now he still maintains our failure to go to England was part of a comprehensive package of reprisals by individuals inside the country working in cahoots with vengeful western governments to reverse the gains of our hard won independence. At the time I remember I discussed the visa issue with my sister Prim on several occasions but, as usual, she would be in one of her foul moods and I could never get anything sensible out of her.

'We have never stopped the white people from coming here, even thought they once made us slaves,' I reasoned.

'So what? That was a long time ago.'

'But it's our sister's wedding, Prim. Benny will not be happy if we are not there. '

'Just go and do your homework.'

I secretly hoped there would be a last-minute hitch and then the event would be indefinitely postponed until our government and the European Union sorted out their problems and we got our visas. But the wedding went like clockwork. Benny sent us the wedding video and over a hundred photographs by e-mail, but although they were quite interesting it was not the same feeling as actually being there in the flesh, toasting the newly-weds and eating a piece of the wedding cake. And Benny looked so incredibly beautiful in her lily-white wedding gown my mother wanted to cry.

'Just look at her,' she sighed, 'floating like an angel.'

Last month Benny sent my mother an e-mail saying she is expecting any time soon. She said she went for a scan and they told her it was a boy. They are going to call him Uhuru, which in Swahili means freedom. Prim said she does not understand why people find out the sex of unborn babies. She says it takes out all the fun out of childbirth. It's like knowing in advance the grades you will get for the O-levels, she argued. As I have already said, Prim is not terribly bright. And we don't need her brain scanned to know what grades she will get for her O-levels.

Because my country is still on the European Union's list of bad guys we cannot go to England to see Benny and the baby, when it eventually comes. As for me, it's bye-bye Piccadilly Circus, bye-bye Big Ben, bye-bye London Zoo, bye-bye Ten Downing Street. And because Benny's papers are still not in order there in England she cannot come here and see us. We will just have to make do with a video and pictures of baby Freedom, just as we had to make do with the video and pictures of the wedding in the big stone church in Cambridge. Perhaps our government and the British will work out their problems. Now, that would be a real win-win situation. But somehow, I don't think it will happen any time soon.

Like my father always says, politics is a dirty game.

Christmas

Bryony Rheam

IT'S A STRANGE FAMILY, OURS, A REAL MIXTURE. I manage to avoid most of them during the year, but not at Christmas. At Christmas they all pop again for the once-a year family dinner. Not that we'll all be together this time. For one, Nicholas and Lisa are in New Zealand. They left in March and live in a place called Wellington. I looked it up in my school atlas; it's very far away. They said to me they'd try and come back for Christmas, but Mom says they're really busy and don't have much money, so she didn't expect them home. They sent us a postcard when they first arrived and I wrote back, but I haven't heard from them since, except when they write to Gran.

Gran, now she's a funny one. Eighty-nine this year and still going strong. That's what she always says, even after her hip replacement operation. We had to go to Joburg for that. Mom and Dad and I took her in the car and we stayed at Auntie Lesley's place in Rivonia. We went last school holidays and stayed the whole four weeks. It was fun, except that Mom had an argument with Auntie Lesley because Mom says no one else helps with Gran and we really can't afford it because we live in Zimbabwe. Dad says our dollar is now worth less than the Zambian Kwacha, and we always used to laugh at the Zambians.

Uncle Peter comes from Zambia. He's always talking about it. Dad calls him a 'whenwe' and rolls his eyes every time Uncle Peter says 'when we were in Zambia'. My sister, Linda, says Zimbabweans are like that in England. 'When we were in Zimbabwe' they always say. She lives in London and works in a shop. She does the till. Dad says why leave Zimbabwe to work in a shop, when you can stay here and

104

have a good job? Linda says it's not that easy because you earn more money working in a shop in London than you do in an office in Zimbabwe. Dad shakes his head and says so why are you living in a house with fifteen other people if you're earning so much money? Linda says that's what Zimbabweans do now; they try and help each other out when they first go over and don't have much money. Dad says why don't they help each other out while they're in Zimbabwe, then they wouldn't have to go to England and all squeeze into one house? Linda throws her arms up and shouts, 'Oh, I give up!'

Linda worked in Macdonald's for a year. That's how she met her boyfriend, Arnie. He's from Australia and he's a bodyguard. Not much up top though, said Mom after last Christmas when he came back with her. Dad said it was like talking to the dog, except at least the dog responded by wagging its tail or pricking up his ears. When you spoke to Arnie, you could see the words taking a while to sink in. We played Trivial Pursuit after Christmas lunch and he didn't even know which state Brisbane is in. Dad said afterwards that that's like not knowing if Bulawayo was in Matabeleland or not. We even gave him two chances. I'm usually the only one who's allowed two chances, and most of the time Mom holds a book up in front of her face and whispers the answers to me from behind it. I won once, like that. But that's because I'm only ten. Arnie's thirty-two.

At first Mom and Dad were worried about the big age gap between Linda and Arnie, but once they met him, Dad said he felt a whole lot better. He was even too thick to cheat. At one point it was his turn to ask questions, and he didn't even look at the answer first, like Johnnie, that's my cousin, does when he plays. Johnnie's a real cheat, but you have to be quick to be a good one and Arnie's certainly not that. Dad says no wonder the guy's a bodyguard, because if he's shot, even in the head, all they have to do is pick him off the floor, give him a bit of a dust over and he'll be OK again. Probably won't notice anything different.

'Typical Aussie,' Dad says, but Mom says that's not nice, she's sure there's some really clever ones. Dad says name one and Mom thinks and says, 'Shane Warne'. 'He's a cricket player,' says Dad. 'What's so clever about him?' 'I don't know,' says Mom. 'Anyway, you must be clever to know where to hit the ball so you make the other players run.'

'He's a bowler,' says Dad. 'Oh,' says Mom, 'well, I don't know then.' Dad went to Australia once on a business trip. Beautiful country, he said. Except for the people who live there, it might be as good as Zimbabwe. Mom said there's a lot of ex-Zimbabweans living there now and Dad got cross and says you're either a Zimbabwean or you're not. You can't be an ex. You can't divorce your country. 'Some people have,' mutters Mom, but he doesn't hear her.

This Christmas, it's going to be quite sad without Pops. He was my Granddad and I know Dad will miss him not being here. Pops died in April. He had a farm out at Nyamandlovu, not a big place, but big enough for someone to want as theirs. We helped him move all his things into town, but knowing he would never return was too much for him. It wasn't just that. Uncle Chook is buried out there, and Pops loved him so much he felt he was leaving him behind.

Uncle Chook's real name was Charles, but no one ever called him that, except his teachers on his school report. Uncle Chook was only eighteen when he was killed. It was the day after he left Plumtree and came back to work on the farm. He was shot by dissidents, once in the head. We have a picture of him on the dresser. It was taken the week before he died.

Julia and Glen are also not with us this Christmas; they're in California. Glen's my cousin Johnnie's brother, and he's married to Julia, a girl he met when he was only sixteen. He's never had another girlfriend. Dad reckons he's a fool not to have played the field a bit before getting hitched, but Mom says it's great; that's what love is, knowing someone is right for you from the start. Dad says every guy should sow his wild oats before he gets married. At first, I thought he meant that every man should be a farmer, but Mom says it's what you say when you think someone should have gone out with a few women before settling down.

I suppose that's what her brother, Uncle Tony, is doing. He's forty-two and he's never been married. He's had lots of girlfriends though, and he's been engaged twice. At the moment, he's got a coloured girl-friend called Delphine. Dad rolled his eyes at first, but now he says she's OK and keeps Uncle Tony under her thumb. It must be quite hard as Uncle Tony is a big guy. He used to play prop for Queens, but now he just props up the bar. Mom's always soft on Tony because he's her little brother. She always sticks up for him, and makes him his favourite meal, steak, egg and chips, when he gets dumped. She makes it quite often and Dad's told her to go easy on the steak.

The last girlfriend he had, Madeline Oosthuisen, left him for

Parkie Monroe. Parkie Monroe's the estate manager at my school. Dad said, 'now there's one picnic short of a sandwich' when he met Parkie. Imagine him and Arnie as a quiz team, he joked to Mom and I. Parkie's always getting into fights, and he's threatened to beat Uncle Tony up before. Uncle Tony came to my school once to watch Old Boys' cricket and Parkie came up to him near the boerewors tent and 'Come, come my boet, let's settle this once and for all.'

Delphine's bringing her brother to lunch today. We don't know what Dad's going to say because Delphine's brother is a man who likes kissing other men. That's what Mom told me anyway. He's not French (French men kiss each other, but that's OK because that's what they've been trained to do since they were children) but he's gay, which doesn't mean he's happy either. Delphine said she's told him not wear eyeliner or earrings, so maybe Dad won't guess. Mom says he can't bring his boyfriend this Christmas. Let's do this one step at a time.

I've decorated the tree and the table and made place names for everybody. Dad inspects the seating arrangements and moves the places of those sitting on either side of him. He doesn't want to sit anywhere near Uncle Peter or Gran. 'Are you trying to kill me?' he asks. 'The last thing I need to hear about on Christmas Day is Lusaka, 1969, or Bloemfontein to Esigodeni by ox wagon.'

'That's my mother you're talking about,' shouts Mom from the kitchen. 'Am I ever allowed to forget it?' mutters Dad to me. To Mom, he calls, 'And what a wonderful woman she is!' Mom comes in and hits him with a tea towel. 'You behave,' she says, 'it's Christmas.'

Mom's doing all the cooking and she looks like she needs a break. Dad tells Linda to help, but she's been out all night at some club and she's exhausted. She sits drinking glass after glass of water and won't move when Mom tells her to go and get ready. 'Why do I have to be smart?' she whines. 'It's just family.'

'Hey,' says Dad in a voice that says move your arse or I'll give you a fat crack. 'The Poms may have lost their standards, but we still have ours.'

Linda's found a new man, a guy from Matsheumhlope, who also lives in London now and they've agreed to meet on Boxing Day. I guess Arnie won't be out here again next Christmas.

Gran arrives first. Well, that's because Dad and I go to fetch her. She lives at Garden Park in a cottage of her own. When we get there, she's already had a few toots with old man de Souza, who lives next door. He's saying, in broken English, that he wants to marry Gran and take her to Lorenco Marques. Dad tells him it's Maputo now, and he's not taking Gran anywhere, she's coming to lunch with us. Gran kisses him good-bye and says 'adios amigo'. Dad says, 'Wrong language, but anyway, get in the car and let's get the hell out of here.'

Then Uncle Peter and Johnnie arrive. They also look like they had a hooley last night. I know that because Uncle Peter says 'just water for me' when Dad asks him what he wants to drink and then Dad does that funny thing with his eyebrows that means 'I give up'. Last year, Johnnie brought his son, Jamie, with him, but this year it's his ex-wife's turn to have him. She's remarried a guy called Pete Parrott. Johnnie says how's that for a name and Dad asks if he's the kind of guy who repeats everything you say. We all laugh. In fact, Mom's cousin, Raymond, used to have a pet parrot that he carried round all day on his shoulder. 'If only I'd known what I was marrying into,' mutters Dad whenever he hears that story.

Uncle Tony arrives with Delphine and Jermaine. Jermaine's not wearing any make-up, but he is carrying a handbag and Dad raises his eyebrows when he sees that. He raises them even more when he sees the rings on Jermaine's fingers and Mom coughs and talks loudly before he has time to say anything.

Two hours later, we all sit down for lunch at last. By now the drinks have been flowing and Uncle Tony's got very loud. He excuses himself from the table, but has to hang on to it while he steadies himself a bit. Mom looks at Dad as if to say why did you give him so much to drink. Dad gives her a look as if to say it's not my fault. He goes to use the toilet next door, although Mom's told him before to use the one down the passage so we don't hear him. Uncle Tony always makes a lot of noise when he goes to the loo. Mom tries to talk loudly, but all we can hear is Uncle Tony taking a leak.

'Jeez,' says Dad.

'It's like Vic Falls,' says Uncle Peter.

Uncle Tony doesn't come back into the dining room and I'm sent to find him, in case he's taken the wrong turning and ended up in Mom and Dad's room. It happened once before and, I can tell you, Dad was not impressed. I find him on the phone in the hallway, calling Madeline. He's telling her how much he loves her and what a mistake he made going off with Delphine. He's forgotten it was Madeline who left him. I go back into the dining room and tell everyone's he's coming. It's best not say what I heard.

Uncle Tony comes back in and Mom starts dishing up. Then his cellphone rings. He can't find it at first, but then he does and he answers it at the table. Mom pulls a face and points outside with her thumb. Uncle Tony ignores her. It's Parkie Monroe. We all know because Uncle Tony starts shouting at him. He ends the call, but it rings again. This time, Delphine answers, much to Tony's horror, and she tells Parkie to stop phoning. Then her face goes black like thunder and she says, 'OK, I'll tell him.' She puts the phone down and turns to Uncle Tony. He's cowering to one side like she's going to hit him with the turkey and she says, 'He says he'll stop phoning you, if you stop phoning her!'

'Her who?' asks Tony in exactly the same kind of voice I use when Mom asks whose eaten all the chocolates she's brought back from South Africa. That's it. Delphine snaps and throws the phone at Uncle Tony. Then she storms out of the room and Uncle Tony runs after her. Jermaine sniggers and rolls his eyes. I can see he's enjoying it. Dad also rolls his eyes, but he's not laughing. 'Only in Bulawayo,' he says.

Mom says to Gran, 'So, how's your new neighbour, Mr de Souza, isn't it?' Dad gives her a look to say 'don't mention Mr de Souza,' but she just looks at him and shrugs. Gran remains tight-lipped. She hasn't forgiven Dad for dragging her away this morning. Uncle Peter starts talking about Zambia and Johnnie helps himself to another drink. Then Delphine and Tony come back in. Delphine looks like she's been crying and Uncle Tony has a large hand mark on one cheek. Ainar! That looks like it hurt! But they're OK and that's the main thing, although I had worked out that I might get a considerable amount more Christmas pudding if she, he and Jermaine had left before lunch started.

We're about to start, but just then the phone rings. Dad sighs and throws down his knife and fork. It's for Linda; it's Arnie, phoning with the last credits left on his phone card after phoning his parents in Sydney – that's Sydney, New South Wales, Arnie. He tells Linda he loves her and she comes and tells us he loves her and she loves him. So I expect we'll see Arnie again sometime.

Then Dad raises his glass and says, 'I'd like to make a toast. To absent friends!' Everyone raises their glasses and says 'To absent friends!' and takes a sip of their drinks. I know Dad's thinking about Nicholas and Lisa in New Zealand and Julia and Glen in California.

He's thinking, too, about Pops and Uncle Chook, so long gone now that he no longer cries for him on his birthday. Dad glances briefly at the photo on the dresser, the one of Uncle Chook in his Plumtree uniform, and he tilts his glass slightly in a toast. I know what he's thinking. He's thinking, 'Cheers Chooky! Cheers Pops! Keep me a cold one!' Then he looks away at Mom opposite him and smiles. Mom smiles, too. She's a little tipsy because she doesn't know Johnnie keeps topping up her glass.

'Great meal, love,' he says and puts a forkful in his mouth.

'Hear, hear,' says Uncle Peter and everyone else murmurs 'hear, hear'. Even Uncle Tony and Delphine and Gran manage a smile, so Mom smiles more. Because she's happy. Because it's Christmas. Once again.